Uncle Tim's
First Year

A Beginner's Guide To The Guitar

By Tim Gillespie

Published by

MOUNTAIN
STUDIOS

Mountain Studios
1025 Oakdale Place
Boulder CO 80304

Uncle Tim's
First Year

A Beginner's Complete Guide to the Guitar

By Tim Gillespie

Published by:

Visualize Great Music

Mountain Studios
1025 Oakdale Place
Boulder CO 80304-0749

First Printing 1998
Second Printing 1999
Third Printing 2000
Fourth Printing 2001
Fifth Printing 2002
Sixth Printing 2006

Printed in the United States

Library of Congress Card Catalog Number 97-092762
ISBN 0-9647059-5-8 $14.95

Thanks Sara!
Thanks Violet!
Thanks T. A.

Table Of Contents

Glossary of Terms

Note. A tone produced by striking a guitar string. Each string is tuned to a note. Each string will produce a note at each fret. Each fret will raise the note one half step.

Frets. The smallest distance you can travel on a fretboard. The metal raised bars extending the entire width of the fretboard. The frets start near the tuning pegs and extend down the fretboard almost to the sound hole of the guitar. Frets are positioned to allow musical notes to be created by pressing the string at any fret and striking the string.

Chord. A minimum of three tones played at the same time. Chords (in this first section) are built by combining every other note in the scale, starting with the note of the chord, until you have three. That way, each note in the scale will have a chord named after it.

Triad. Three notes. The simplest chord available. The smallest possible combination of notes (three) necessary to form a chord. Triads can be major, minor, diminished or augmented. Advanced forms are also possible.

Strumming. Strumming is the basic right or pick hand technique for a right handed guitarist. Strumming is the process of repeatedly striking some or all of the strings in an effort to create a rhythm while holding down a chord with the fretboard hand.

Picking. The right hand technique of striking individual strings to sound a series of individual notes.

Plectrum Style. Finger picking using only the fingers. Usually a combination of the thumb and at least one finger (often times two or three fingers). Using a plectrum style a guitarist can play the guitar without a pick.

Octave. The distance traveled to sound the second occurrence of the same note. The distance between C and the next C. In the example of do re mi fa so la ti do, do's represent the octave.

Open String Note. The note sounded by striking a guitar string without pressing it down at a fret. The note each string is tuned to.

Sharp. Raising a note one fret. If you raise a G one fret it becomes a G#. If you raise it one more fret it becomes an A.

Flat. Lowering a note one fret. If you lower an A note one fret it becomes a Ab. If you lower it one more fret it becomes a G.

Enharmonic Spelling. A second way of saying the same thing. An Ab is the same thing as a G#. It is the exact same note but it has two names.

You will see more in depth definitions as you get farther along. As you see more examples of each, you will start to understand the meanings in context.

Throw away all your fears about learning and just enjoy the journey.
When you do that, you pass through the greatest barrier.

It does not matter where you start the journey, everyone will begin from a different starting point.
What matters is what you do with your time, and where you aim.

If you are willing to work, you will end up where you want to go.
Figure out what you want and make sure it is what you want, because that is where you will go!

Hello!

Welcome to Uncle Tim's First Year. This book is all about exploring the guitar for the first time. Of the books I have written, I found this to be the most difficult. Since it is a beginner book it might seem reasonable that this would be the easiest one to write. The difficulty arose from trying to determine how much of the fundamentals a person new to the guitar should learn and how much time should be spent just playing. The purpose of this book is to teach you only what is necessary so that you may concentrate on playing.

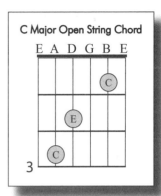

C Major Open String Chord

The guitar is a very rich instrument. There are many things you can do with it. Because the guitar is so rich, it cannot help but be complex. Presenting a simplified view can make it easier for the student but often at the expense of the lesson under study. In some ways it is not the right thing to do. Part of learning is understanding the basis of the information. You must be able to see into issues and form your own opinion if you are going to breathe life into this. However, learning should be approached in a simple way. I want to eliminate all the distractions and concentrate on what is most important. I have attempted to blend a broad range of information and good exercise in this book. By reading and playing, the physical act will reinforce the mental lesson. You will start to answer your own questions. In other words if you play along and think a little, you should expect to learn! At first the chord fingerings are simple, they will get more complex as you get farther along. The scales will also be simple. **By playing the chords and scales of each key you become musically grounded. This will become the basement of your foundation! It will bear great weight!**

You become better by playing, but you must know what to play. This book will provide the important aspects of what you really should know. It is my intention to keep it simple but provide meaningful lessons that will provide the foundation for many years of growth. **This should not be difficult but it is very serious. Expect serious results!**

From the chords we learn, will come the ability to play songs.

From the scales we learn, will come the emotional melodic statements of lead guitar.

From the structured passage of time and effort, will come a strong, unshakable foundation of competence and ability!

Are Scales Really Necessary?

Have you ever noticed that almost every good music teacher for any stringed instrument includes scales in their program? Do you think that is a coincidence?

Close Your Eyes - What Do You See For Yourself

When I think back to what I wanted when I decided to learn to play guitar, I always pictured a smooth fluid performer able to switch styles and play a wide variety of songs. I wanted to evoke an emotional response from my music. How do you get there from here? What is it that allows a person to get so good? How do you teach someone to be able to rip off a lead in the middle of a jam session, having never played the song before?

My Own Personal Experience

I decided I would learn to read music right away. I picked an easy song and tried to read it. I read the music and played it. After several hours you could begin to hear a faint melody, however, I did not survive the process. I went back to try again and again, but got no farther. This approach did not work for me. I was spending too much time learning to read music and not enough time exercising my fingers. It was not fun. I felt lost. Several months later I tried it again in about the same way and got the same result. The instrument sat for another year. After awhile, I didn't even tune it.

After Several Failed Attempts

Several months later I was at a friend's house. He was trying to become a lead singer and his playing partner was an accomplished guitarist. I sat around watching them play some rock and I saw my first movable chord. When I saw that chord moved to three different positions, I realized how things worked. I rushed home to play that chord. I played it and moved it. I concentrated on clamping down on all the strings and hearing the notes. **I played and moved that chord until my hands ached. My hands ached for the very first time. They have been killing me ever since!**

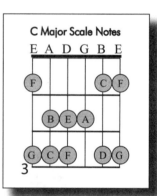

In hindsight I realized that it was to hard to do all the things that my previous approach asked of me. Several things had to be done at the same time. I had to read the music, figure out what strings to press, press them down and go to the next chord and repeat the process. Miss any part of that process and the whole thing comes to a grinding halt. Spending so much time on something that was a secondary goal (learning to read music) interrupted the experience of playing the guitar. Feedback was a dribble, doubts were generated and somewhere in the process my commitment wavered. Next thing I knew the guitar was in the closet, and I was off to another hobby. I didn't even realize it when it happened!

I was interested in playing music, but I was trying to do too many other things. By focusing on what was necessary, I could progress right away. Reading music is important and beneficial. But using it as the only way I interfaced with the guitar was not a good idea. I wanted to concentrate on getting the feel of the guitar. I just needed a way to get my hands and head involved. When I did that, I became a guitar player in a few weeks. Then reading music made much more sense to me.

Get To Know Your Body

It is normal to experience some cramping and discomfort as your body undertakes the demands of playing a guitar. However, this should go away with a small amount of rest. If you experience lingering pain it may be advisable to regulate your time and make sure your body is reacting normally.

How Do You Learn To Play A Guitar?

This book addresses the issues necessary to play the guitar. It is centered around fundamental skills you should acquire in the first year. The direction you choose is based on the music you like. If you want to play pop or rock music, this book contains the information necessary for that music. If you want to play jazz, country or other demanding styles, you must first be able to play the material presented here. If you want to write songs, you must know something about keys. As you get beyond the entry level stages of the instrument you will be able to adjust your course based on what you have learned and your new skills! You get these skills by developing a structured routine and thinking about what you are doing. You will go beyond a person that only plays a couple of chords in a matter of weeks.

I believe it is important to give people good, solid information at an easy, steady pace. This book is meant to be read several times, because that is how people really learn. You will not understand everything right away. You need continued exposure and to know why it is necessary to learn something. If motivated, most people can learn what they want. One of the reasons to play chord and scale exercises is so you can play passages based on them. When the time comes, you already know what to do.

It Is Impossible To Play Correctly
If You Are Not Sure Of What You Are Playing

To become a guitar player you must put in time and develop the ability to control the instrument. Start by learning some easy chords. Everyday you will get a little farther. Sometimes big explosions of growth occur and it can be exciting. If you play for at least an hour a day, you can become a guitarist in as little as three months. No one will have to tell you exactly when it happens. You will know. You will hear it when you play. The results will not show up until you put in some work, but if you do, they will show up. It is the same for everyone, this is how we learn. Put in the work then get the reward.

Three Chords In C Major

Here are three chords in C major. The picture shows you what the chords look like. The graphic below is the standard way chords will be presented.

Once you get used to chord charts, you will be able to play songs using chords. If you want to play them now, give it a try. Look at the picture to see what fingers to use. Play all the strings, except those covered by a black dot.

C Major

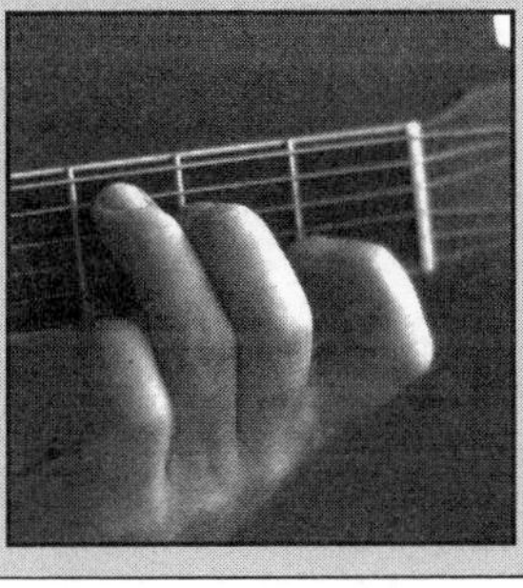

F Major

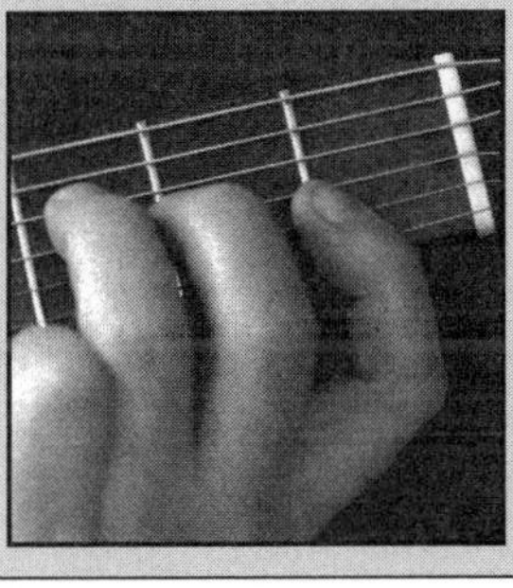

G Major

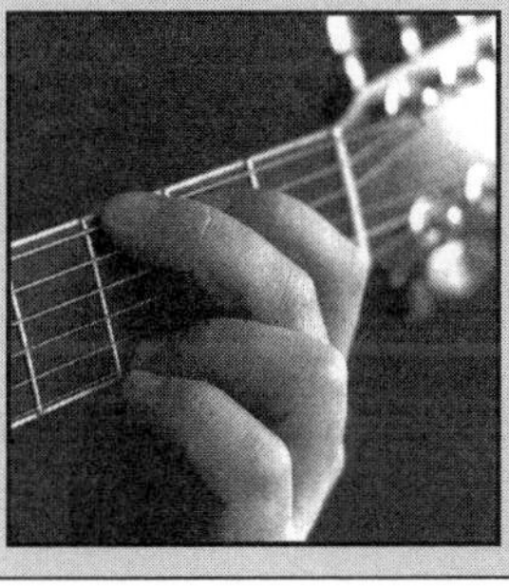

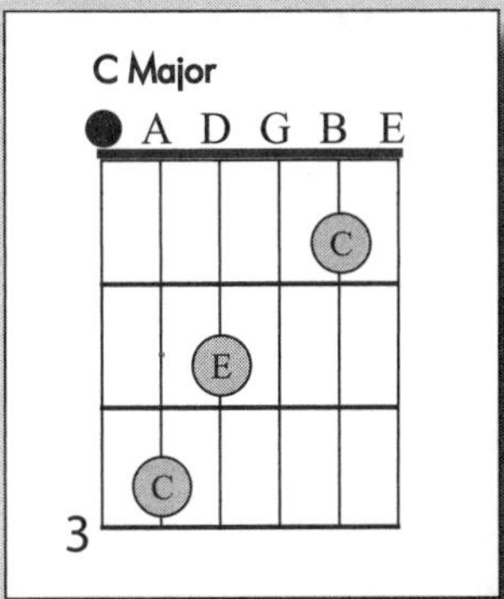

C Major
● A D G B E
C
E
C
3

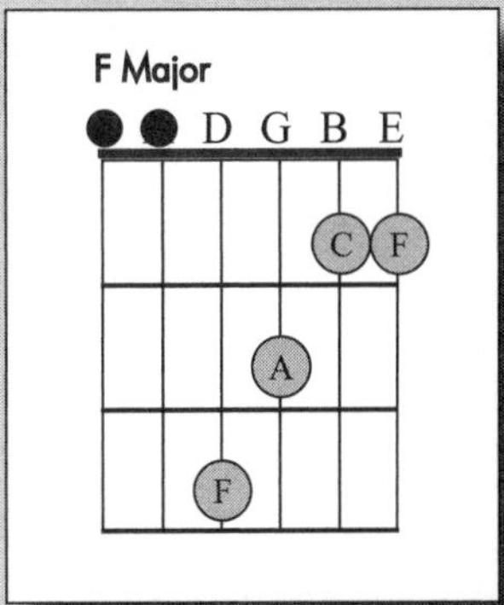

F Major
● ● D G B E
C F
A
F

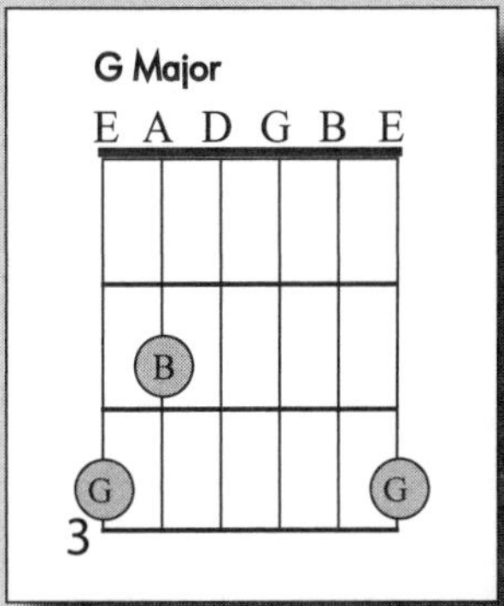

G Major
E A D G B E
B
G   G
3

My Experience

Artistic And Technical Skills

There are two kinds of skills required to play a guitar. Artistic skills and technical skills. Artistic skills include playing songs and performing. Technical skills include sounding notes, moving your hands to a new position, finger picking and other mechanical concepts. **In order for artistic skills to come forth, some technical skills must be in place. The more technical skills present, the greater freedom you have to express your artistic side.** Technical skills include learning how to physically play the instrument, which fingers to use, where to place them and how to strike the strings. Artistic skills involve understanding what it is that you want to say and transforming notes and exercises into music. You must be able to execute what it is that you want to play. Mechanical skills support artistic skills.

My First Year

My first year (after my failures) was a typical experience with a few notable exceptions. Those exceptions allowed me to get much better in a very short time. I could tell I was getting better because people would start to notice and comment. It felt different. When I would create a secondary part in a jam session, people asked me how I did it.

Like most people I learned a few songs. Actually parts of songs, the parts I liked. In the beginning I learned some chords so I could play along with everyone else. And I learned to copy a few lead lines but not very well! My fingers had trouble with anything difficult. I was not very strong. When I experimented with chord progressions I did not know why one chord worked and another did not. My creative sparks were limited by my lack of understanding. A big frustration set in.

Scales

The biggest change occurred when I decided to study scales. I did so because I went in a music store and some guy was ripping off leads. I asked him how I could do that and he handed me a scale book. I started to read musical notation again. But this time it was different. I was not trying to learn by reading only. I already knew how to play. Make no mistake reading has enormous benefits, but by learning to read at the same time you are trying to learn to form chords and play songs, another big level of complexity is added.

By playing scales I was learning on a variety of levels. Levels that got more interesting as I continued to play. On a basic level I began to really understand the movement of fingers across strings, because my fingers were constantly moving. I also began to fill in some mental blanks. I realized that all the notes for the key of C are C, D, E, F, G, A and B. If I wanted to play in the key of C, those were the only notes I could use. I would listen to the radio and once I figured out the key of a song, I could figure out the chords or the lead lines. After a while I could create my own lead lines. That is when I really noticed the benefits of playing scales.

This Is Not A Secret Method

This book is based on common sense information that forms the skills necessary to play the guitar. It is not a secret but it will lead to a comprehensive strategy. It is the information necessary to understand the basics shown in a simple but complete way. The strategy will be revealed as we go, but you need some information before we can visualize it! There are some remarkably easy ways of understanding giant concepts, keep reading.

A Structured Approach

Set Up A Schedule

My advice is this, keep it simple but do not shy away from learning. Get to know the feel of a guitar and put in practice hours. You can control how long it takes to become a guitarist by how long you practice. If you practice one hour a day, it will take between three to nine months for the muscles in your hands and arms to control the guitar. If you practice for a couple of hours a day, it can be done in a shorter amount of time. After several months I developed a three hour daily schedule which I used for a few years. Here is an outline of my first structured schedule. Keep in mind that schedules can change as a part of your lifestyle.

The First Part. Scales! I would start out in the key of C and play the scales right next to the nut of a guitar (the same scales in this book). The nut is where the strings leave the fretboard and go into the tuning pegs. Then I would go to the key of G, then A, then E and so on. Starting with C and continuing through the circle of fifths. Play it this way and you gradually add difficulty. The first hour made my hands ache because scales will exercise your entire hand and make you work to play them correctly. **That exercise will jump start your ability to coordinate your fingers. You will see it in a few pages.**

The Second Part. I would then play an hour of chords. Starting with the easiest ones and working up to the harder ones. Every week I would add a couple of new chords. I would practice passages and isolate the areas that I found difficult. I would break down my finger motions. Since I was studying scales and keys, I really had a good idea of what basic chords worked in each key. I would change chords very slowly and make sure I was hitting all notes as cleanly as possible (most of the time).

The Third Part. I would then play all the songs I knew. I would go through the chord charts on written songs and try to play the chords. Sometimes I would need help, other times I could get it by myself. If I met a guitarist that knew a song I wanted to learn, I would show him (or her) something of interest. This usually guaranteed I would get the opportunity to learn something new.

You do not have to practice for three hours a day. But whatever amount you do choose, dividing it like this can break up the day into structured groups assuring you that the fundamentals will be addressed. The benefits of a structured practice schedule are enormous! With the passage of time this will make a huge difference in the abilities you develop.

If you do choose to practice a couple of hours a day, I strongly suggest you consider getting a teacher. A good instructor should eliminate the possibility of developing poor habits and wasted time.

Different Forms of D Major

These chords are both D major. We have added a D and F# note to the bottom chord to change the look and sound of it. It is still a D major chord. Play them and see.

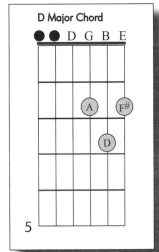

D Major Chord

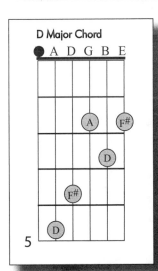

D Major Chord

Habits - Technique

Habits can be either good or bad. Good habits will allow you to build on your current level of ability and properly position yourself for future growth. If you have good habits, you do not have to overcome artificial limitations that bad habits can impose. **If you develop good habits, you should expect to improve.**

Bad habits can severely limit your ability to obtain higher levels of skill. Here is an example. If you use only two fingers to play scales, you will have a difficult time playing fast guitar parts, because using four fingers can be more efficient. It does not mean that you cannot overcome the limitations of the technique, but you will be forced to put energy into overcoming it. That mental and physical energy could be directed in something much more productive. There are plenty of examples and you may not be able to recover from some of them. That is why it is a good idea to learn correctly the first time. Usually it is no harder to learn correctly than to learn the wrong way. If you develop good technique it will continue to help you, if you develop bad technique you may have to unlearn it later or learn to live with it.

There is one habit that I learned early and it makes some things easier and some things harder. There is a picture of this coming up. I play an open G chord and allow my thumb to slip from the center ridge and ride up by the low E string. It forces me to keep the palm of my hand against the neck. This prevents me from being in the proper position to play a lead after the chord in some instances. This technique is commonly used. It will not stop you but it may make it harder and it may impose a limit.

Instructors

It is best to choose an instructor based on your needs. This may sound simple but it can be confusing. Instructors will all be different. Some are generalists and some will offer specific instruction based on their skills. It is possible to pick a very good instructor but the wrong one for you. Choose one that will take you in the direction you want to go. Do not blindly trust an instructor to teach you what you want. Be a partner in the process! Good instructors can help you but remember you are the manager of your own future. Make sure the instructor you choose has a clear understanding of what you want and can show you how to get there. That is the reason you go to an instructor in the first place. **Expect results!**

My idea of a good instructor is one who has the correct answers and can help you to understand it, both physically and mentally. Good answers are helpful in solving persistent problems. The easier the answer is to understand, the better the instructor. If you understand what you want to learn or can at least describe it, you stand a better chance of picking the right instructor to teach it. Sharing ideas and building trust can ensure both you and the instructor have a rewarding experience.

I have had several different instructors, sometimes for a specific purpose and sometimes for general studies over extended periods. The right instructor can bring positive change right away. I have used a voice instructor that almost always had the right answer right away, (because he really understands voice) and it always helped me. It was remarkable how that instructor could remove mental road blocks that were limiting my progress! The hardest part was thinking of the right questions to ask.

Getting Started

Remember, You Are In Charge!

It is always the practice that teaches you the meaning of the concepts under study. As you play, a gradual, clear understanding will emerge and take shape. The learning comes from repetition and thinking about what you are doing. Develop exercises that test your ability to change chords and play scales with no mistakes. Play the chords and scales over and over. At times you should press yourself to play the scales slightly louder than normal and with as much physical control as you can exert. Play in control but extend your limits of clarity, tone and physical control. **In short, take control! Even if you have very little musical talent, practice will make up for almost all of it. Almost everyone should be able to do this. The secret is work and practice!**

How To Use This Book

1. We examine the Fretboard and make sure we understand how it works as well as some basic concepts. You will have several chances to get these concepts, do not worry if some concepts seem disconnected.

2. We examine technique for holding the guitar, strumming and picking the guitar. You have to be able to hold it comfortably.

3. We will play the scales and chords for all twelve diatonic keys. For starters just play the notes of the scale up and down and play the chords, 1 through 6 as shown. Don't worry about anything else, just play the chords and scales. Play the progression of chords at least 50 times for each key. Play the scales non stop for several 10 minutes sessions (or as close to 10 minutes sessions as possible). Concentrate on only one key for the first few weeks. Later you can go to the next. Be patient, you will know them all in a few months.

4. Read the text. All of it! You do not have to do this first, or read it every time. It is all right to turn off the mental approach and concentrate on just playing, however, there must be times when the mental approach is in use while playing. Try to make some sense of everything as you go, and it will fall into place. Sometimes rereading the concepts will help. It takes time. Do not rush this.

You get better by playing songs, chords and scales over and over. You must play this material over and over again. Everyone who learned to play a guitar, repeated what they learned countless times. Repetition is the key. It is the only way to teach your fingers. Remember to pick and play some easy songs (more on that later).

What To Do If You Feel Lost!

Sooner or later everyone will feel lost. You may feel like you don't get it or you are not sure if you are learning. When you feel lost, here are some suggestions.

1. Remember you have a structured program that will last at least 6 months. If you complete the program you will be covering the basics. That is something you can rely on. Stick to it and put in quality time and try not to worry.
2. Sometimes the direction you are taking does not yield the results you want. Why? Here are some reasons.
a. It takes time! Change does not happen at once. You must put in the work and as you play, you will become more comfortable. My advice is to work through this. You can even increase practice time. Remember the more you practice the quicker it happens. This is always true.
b. Your mind has not sorted out what you are learning yet. You may understand it but doing it is different.
3. You may want to try practicing with someone. Often the presence of someone else (hopefully better than you) will greatly help. It may give you a chance to see the principles in action. Sometimes it sounds better when someone else is playing it.
4. If all else fails, turn off your brain and just go play without thinking about anything. Just play your guitar.
5. Mix up your schedule to inject some new component. Make sure there is an element of fun. Learn some new songs.
6. Never ever stop playing your guitar, you can work out of anything. We all have had to work through these difficult experiences at one time or another.

Reasonable Expectations

What Will You Know In One Year?

Quite a bit! Here are some of the major accomplishments you should expect.

Chords. A major through G major and all the minors, and some easy seventh chords. You will know several ways to play different chords including barre chords (barring more than one string with one finger).

Scales. For all 12 diatonic and pentatonic keys for the first position. The first position is the area right around the nut and tuning pegs. You will understand how the circle of fifths determines the order of scales and the differences between each scale.

Strumming. You will be able to strum chord progressions and play along with songs in any key.

Finger picking. You should be able to finger pick the chords you know and combine them to play progressions in a key.

Flat picking. You should be able to flat pick chords and start to mix them with lead passages. Flat picking can take some time to master.

Songs. Somewhere around 20 or more, depending on how many you pick and what type of ratio between practicing chords and scales and playing songs you establish. Don't worry if your song count is lower.

Knowledge of all the notes and common chords in all twelve keys and how to apply it to musical situations. You will begin to understand how keys relate to one another and why we place such importance on them. You will be able to enter a jam session and have a understanding of how the music flows. You will be able to play some lead guitar and use the common chords to play rhythm. You may hear a song on the radio and be able to understand how it was created and pick it off the record. This will be due to your knowledge of keys.

Timing. You should be able to keep time in simple songs. Practicing with a metronome will enforce your ability to keep time.

Reading music. You will be able to read chord charts, and play chords and scales based on musical notation.

You will also begin to understand the repetitive nature of the guitar and how any chord can be moved to become a different chord while maintaining the same form. You will begin to understand that scales will behave the same way.

In short, you will have an understanding of the fundamentals of playing. You will be ready to direct your interest to what you like and take your music in your own direction confidently. You will also be ready to take the next steps to fully understand music. When you finish Uncle Tim's First Year, you will have memorized almost everything necessary to understand Uncle Tim's Building Blocks. That is no small feat. Then you just have to learn how to use it.

How Guitar Strings Work

Guitar strings behave the same way all strings do. You tune them to a note so that when you strike the string, you sound that note. The distance between that note and the next is a matter of physics. Notice there are sharps between some notes and not others. The smallest increment on a guitar is a fret. Except for bending notes or special effects, the smallest distance you can travel is a fret. The frets of a guitar are spaced so that each fret will allow a single note to be sounded by depressing the string there. Remember, there are twelve different notes. By sounding a note every fret, you would begin to repeat after twelve frets. That is why the guitar repeats every twelve frets. If you look at your guitar you may notice the fret spacing is always changing. The location of the fret is determined so that when you press any string down, you get a note. Violins do not have frets. The musician must know exactly where to press down on the string. That is one reason why the violin is harder to play than the guitar.

The Spacing Of Notes

Between certain notes there are no frets. The examples are B and C and E and F. All other non sharped notes have a fret between them. No matter how you tune a guitar, this will always be the case. The starting note may be different but the relationship between notes will always be this way. It is the physics of a string that make it happen. All strings will behave the same way for every instrument.

Diatonic Keys

Remember that diatonic keys will split the twelve chromatic notes into seven positions. Each note available (all twelve) will be the keynote for one key. But each key will have only seven notes. Starting with the keynote, they will all have the same spacing. The spacing starting on the keynote, will always be whole step, whole step, half step, whole step, whole step, whole step, half step. You will see some examples throughout this book.

Scales Contain The Notes Of The Key

All the notes in any key will be present in the scale for that key. The example to the right contains all the notes on the string, and all the notes of the key of C for the same string. Each one of these notes will spawn a chord. For the key of C there are chords based on the C, D, E, F, G, A and B notes. To construct these chords, you will use only the scale of C. Chords are built by selecting the first, third and fifth note of the scale starting on the note of the chord. We will build the key of C so you can see this in a few pages.

The 12 notes of the Chromatic scale and the 7 notes of the diatonic key

Everything On A Guitar Repeats

Remember, after you travel twelve frets you start to repeat notes in order. Everything on a guitar repeats every twelve frets. You will see a chord called an F chord and then moved one fret and called an F# chord. It is the same chord form played one fret higher and we know one fret above an F is an F#. Try to remember this because you will see it happen often. This is a major tool in understanding the fretboard.

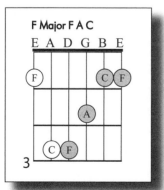

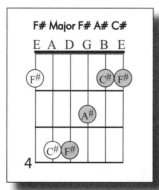

Chord Extensions

You will see chords played several different ways. Chords can be changed by adding notes. We will use the F major and F# major chords as examples. F major has three notes. They are F, A and C. The white circles are F and C notes that can be added to extend the same chord.

The White Dots

On the side of the guitar you will see some small white dots (see picture on page 18). They coincide with the white dots on the fretboard face as shown here. On acoustic guitars these dots usually are placed on the fifth, seventh, ninth and twelfth frets. The twelfth fret may have two dots on the side.

Some classic guitars have dots on the fifth, seventh, tenth and twelfth frets.

These dots are there to serve you as a frame of reference. They help you to orient yourself. Usually they are white dots but they can be dark dots on a light fretboard.

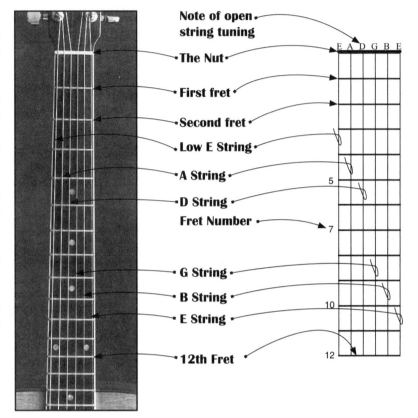

Note of open string tuning
The Nut
First fret
Second fret
Low E String
A String
D String
Fret Number
G String
B String
E String
12th Fret

Using Graphics To Diagram The Fretboard. Once you understand how graphics diagram the fretboard, you can map out the chords, scales and keys easily. Make sure you understand how to read the graphic. The circles show the note on the string at a fret (shown below). Usually we are showing only the notes in a key.

Steps - The Distances Between Frets

There are a couple of different ways to talk about distances. You can talk about the distance between frets as a half step or a whole step. Or you can reference the degrees of the key. Degrees of the scale are referred to by numbers.

Notes   C D E F G A B C
Degrees 1 2 3 4 5 6 7 1

Moving one frets is one half step.

Moving two frets is one whole step.

Moving three frets is one and one half steps.

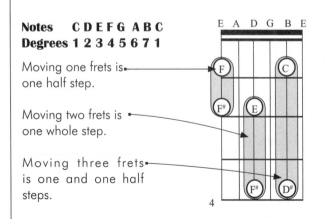

Intervals - The Distances Between Notes In A Key

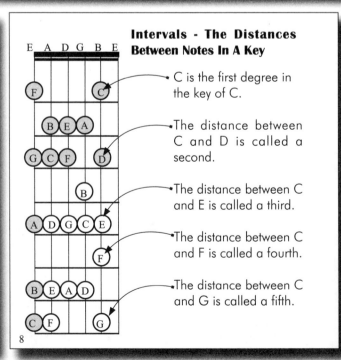

C is the first degree in the key of C.

The distance between C and D is called a second.

The distance between C and E is called a third.

The distance between C and F is called a fourth.

The distance between C and G is called a fifth.

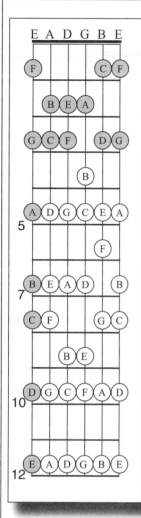

Movement On The Fretboard

If you look in my other books you will see a page like this page in every one. Movement across the fretboard is the essence of playing a guitar. When you play a guitar, one of your hands is always moving. You change chords by moving your fingers. Let's start by noting that there are only twelve notes to play on a guitar. But there are several places to play these twelve notes. Here is what you should know. Look at the graphic on the left. Using the left hand E string only (the lowest), notice the notes are E, F, G, A, B, C, D and E. They are shaded. Now look to the graphic to the right side. Notice that the progression of notes from left to right is the same. Start with the low E string, play the F and G notes. Switch to the A string, play the A open then the B and C notes. On the D string play the D open then the E and F notes. On the G string play the G open then the A note. On the B string play the B open then the C and D notes. Switch to the high E string (all the way to the right) and play the open E then the F and G notes. Look at the notes you just played, they are E̲, F, G, A̲, B, C, D̲, E, F, G̲, A, B̲, C, D, E̲, F and G. Open strings are underlined. You climbed the scale just like when you played the notes on the lower E string. There is one difference, by playing across the strings you were able to play two octaves and three notes. By playing the E string you can only play one octave in twelve frets.

Both paths are important. For the first year we stay around the first five frets. However you will have need to climb up the strings at times. For now just realize there are several ways to move around, we will explore them as we play the chords and scales later.

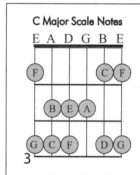

C Major Scale Notes

What Happens When You Change Keys?

Each key will use slightly different notes to make up the key. By selecting only the notes in the key you are working in that key. Notice the white notes are the notes in each key. All twelve notes are shown in each example, but the notes in each key are shown in white. All of these examples use the open string notes.

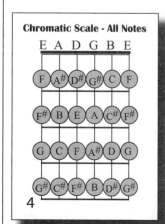

Chromatic Scale - All Notes

Key Of C - No Sharps

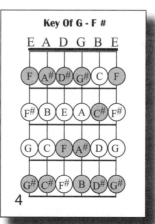

Key Of G - F #

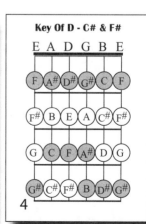

Key Of D - C# & F#

Holding The Guitar

The idea is to make this as easy as possible. After you play for a while you may change the way you hold the instrument, but this is meant to put your hands in position to easily handle the changes as they come. At first it may be uncomfortable to hold the guitar, as you practice it will seem more natural. You may need to alter the form to suit your particular body. Everyone will be somewhat different.

The Electric Guitar

Notice the left hand (fretboard) can easily bend to form this common barre chord. The neck of the guitar is angled to allow the fretboard hand to press any or all six strings. The elbow is in position to support new hand movements. Usually the elbow is forming an angle less than 90 degrees.

Standing up as opposed to sitting down will introduce new dynamics. You may be able to play some things sitting down that become too hard when you are standing. If you practice playing while standing up, it will help you to become more comfortable doing so.

Standing With The Acoustic Guitar

Notice the picking hand is ready to either flat pick or strum. See the glossary at the front of the book or turn to page 44. The fretboard hand can move up, down or across the fretboard to do whatever is necessary.

When you hold a guitar this way the strap is doing most of the work. It can make it easier to concentrate on the fingering if you let the strap support the weight of the instrument.

Straps

Straps can either help you position the guitar for maximum comfort or get in your way. You may have to test a few to determine how thick or thin you like them and how they attach.

The strap in this picture attaches where the guitar body and fretboard meet. Other straps attach at the tuning pegs. It is easier for me to use a strap as shown here. Some straps that attach at the tuning pegs can get in the way. Sometimes this difficulty will go away after you get used to using it.

The weight of the guitar is either transferred to the strap or to your leg. You are holding the guitar by your fingers and thumb, do not try to hold the weight. Think of it as cradling the guitar. Your hands should come around the instrument comfortably.

Sitting With The Guitar

There are two different ways to sit with a guitar. You will probably prefer one of these ways over the others. The biggest difference is the leg holding up the guitar. In the classical style, a guitarist uses a stool to elevate the foot. This in turn changes the angle of the fretboard to the ground by raising the knee. This will allow you to reach the fretboard without lowering your shoulder.

The Classic Position

The leg is elevated and the fretboard is at the optimum angle. Notice the elbow is away from your body and the hand is in position to form chords or single notes.

When you sit with a guitar you balance it as well as hold it. You may or may not use a strap. Much of the time the fretboard hand is only touching the guitar with four fingers and a thumb. The picking or strumming hand is often moving. At first your strumming may bump the instrument. Changing chords becomes hard because the neck is moving when you strum.

The Acoustic Position

You can also sit with the guitar on the other leg. This position makes it harder to hold the guitar and your fretboard hand has a slightly longer reach. Your picking hand is also farther back as the instrument is held to one side of the body.

This can be a comfortable position but you do lose some mobility since you have to work harder to get your hands in position. When getting started, this position contains more compromises and is generally a little more difficult. At first it may be more comfortable holding the guitar in the classical style.

Posture

Your sitting posture should allow for proper hand positioning. Sitting and strumming is the easiest way to play. Sometimes you find it difficult to see the guitar as you play.

You can use the white dots on the side of the neck to orientate yourself. You can slightly rotate

the neck to get a better view but usually only to see a short passage. It is more important to concentrate on feeling the change as you play rather than seeing it. Making a picture of the change in your mind can be very helpful. You can only pass the test of playing in the dark if you play by feel. At first you may need to look at the guitar when you play it.

The Fretboard Hand

Thumb Position

Notice the position of the thumb in relation to the ridge of the guitar. Usually the thumb will rest on the ridge of the guitar which will set the distance between your palm and the Fretboard as shown. Notice the thumb rides the ridge almost directly behind the second finger. This will allow you to exert maximum pressure on the strings.

If you anchor your thumb and keep it in the same position, you will be able to change between chords and single note passages easily. **The technique of the fretboard hand starts with the thumb position.** All hand movements will be shaped by how you hold your thumb. My advice is to anchor the thumb and get your fingers used to changing and hitting chords. All chords and scales start with your hand in the same position. When you ascend or descend, your thumb rides the ridge. Wrapping your thumb will not mean you cannot become a fine guitarist, but you may have to learn a few tricks to compensate. Most guitarists will move their thumb back and forth at least a little. Whatever you decide, make it an informed decision and understand the dynamics. This is a big decision!

Managing Fatigue

One of the first things practicing scales will do is increase your hand strength. Scales will aid that goal very quickly. When you play longer than you are able, you will lose control in your fretboard hand because your muscles cannot press the strings down. This is caused by fatigue. This will test your hand strength which will get better as you build up through practice.

It is very helpful to try to minimize motions so that you do not have to use more energy than is required. We will discuss ways to minimize the output of energy as we progress, one way is to keep your thumb behind the second finger and use it as a perch from which to initiate all movement.

One Finger For Each Fret

In this picture you can see the advantage of assigning one finger to each fret whenever possible. The index finger is responsible for the notes on the second fret. The second finger is playing notes on the third fret and the ring finger is playing notes on the fourth fret. The pinky is playing notes on the fifth fret. The thumb is riding the ridge on the back of the fretboard.

Notice there is almost no stretch required to do this. You can play for a longer period of time if you keep the stretching down, however that is not always possible.

Hit the note either directly behind the fret or towards the middle of the space between frets. If you stay within this area, you will maximize both physical control and tone quality.

The Fretboard Hand

The Five Fret Stretch

Here is an example of stretching your fingers to span more frets. Notice the index finger is playing notes on the third fret, the middle finger is playing notes on the fifth fret and the pinky is playing note on the seventh fret.

In this example the ring finger is not playing any notes. Diatonic scales will require this stretch. Although it takes more energy than using one finger per fret, it is really important to learn to stretch. We will not learn it right away but as we play deeper into the circle of fifths it will become necessary. It is a little harder at first but very necessary. For most people this stretch and this exact fingering is the best choice. You may not think you can do it right away, but it will become much easier after a few weeks. Don't worry about the ring finger, it will become extensively involved.

Linear Playing

Playing a continuous stream of notes requires a different technique than chording. This is facilitated by scales. A stretch like this will be required in the key of Bb. Spans like this require quite a bit of hand strength, this strength is built up as you play the easier scales. By the time you get to the key of Bb you should be able to hold this stretch.

Trying To Get Better?

Look at the strength that this position requires. By making up exercises using this stretching, you cannot help but build up hand strength. As you master the basics of playing scales, you will develop deep strength in your hands. That strength will allow you to get better and do other things.

Finger Tips

The finger tips are the tools for forming chords and plucking strings. For the first few weeks it may hurt your fingers to play. Until you play for a week or so you will have sore, tender fingertips. As you put in the first ten to twenty hours you will start to develop a callus on each finger tip. A callus is a hardened thickened mass of flesh that will protect your fingers from the strings. A callus will change with the amount of time you spend playing. It will get harder with more time and can get soft if you slow down or go on vacation. You can tell if a person plays regularly by examining their calluses. If not for the calluses, these indentations would hurt. With calluses they do not cause any discomfort.

For the first few weeks, moderation is the best course. If you play too hard or long before you have built up calluses, tiny but painful blisters can develop deep within the finger tip. It will be very painful to play while a blister is present. Moderate ramping up of playing time will usually protect you from this. Sometimes a callus will peel off and you must start over with that finger.

Thumb Position

Everything starts with the thumb position. The thumb will dictate the position for the rest of the hand. Many guitarists wrap their thumb around the fretboard and must find a way to overcome the limitations this form imposes. Notice the thumb is quite far from the ridge of the guitar and almost hitting the low E string. If you want to play the next note or chord, you will almost always have to move your thumb to a new position to apply the necessary pressure. This can impose a performance hit. However that said, many people use this position for at least some chords, myself included.

What Happens With This Technique?

Notice the thumb is nowhere near the ridge of the guitar and causes several things to happen. The muscle group used to play this chord is different than the group used in the next picture.

Notice the palm of the hand is smashed against the neck. This imposes a limitation on the finger reach. If you wanted to play a lead right now, you might have to move your thumb to the ridge of the guitar to hit some notes, particularly on the high E string. That means you would have to change this technique before you could go on with the song or figure out some way to hit the strings correctly while maintaining this form.

Riding The Ridge

Although not visible, the thumb is riding the ridge of the neck and there is a space between your palm and the neck. If you need to move, you can do so immediately without moving your palm or your thumb. The fingers are away from the neck and poised to strike any note as needed.

Make no mistake about it. The first picture is a very strong habit. This is a habit I developed and still use from time to time. There are many fine guitarists that extend the thumb over the neck as in the first picture. When playing chords only, it feels comfortable, however it is difficult to play demanding leads with the thumb extended. Pay attention as you form a habit.

How Far Should You Go

Somewhere you may see someone use their thumb to actually hold down a note. While that may be helpful, the performance hit you take for playing that way will cost you more than it can help you. Avoid it if you can at least for the first year. It is an easy habit to pick up and a hard one to get rid of.

The Right Hand

Many people do not realize how much work the right hand does. Right hand technique can make a huge difference in your ability. If you can flat pick, finger pick, strum and play single note passages you have many different ways of sounding the strings. This will create a great advantage. It takes time to learn how to control your hand so you can do all this. But it will give you great control and allow you to combine techniques to add variety.

Finger Picking Position

When finger picking without a pick, I like to use this technique. The thumb is responsible for hitting the three base strings (one at a time) and the index, middle and ring finger are responsible for one treble string each.

Notice the pictures show the three fingers touching one string each. A good way to get comfortable with this method is to pluck four strings at the same time while holding down a chord. Although you are plucking all the strings at the same time you can still feel each string.

Playing simple arpeggios is a good exercise. Play the base notes with the thumb and the other notes with the fingers in order. Pluck the strings one at a time. After you learn a few patterns , you can then mix patterns and switch between them to add interest. Finger picking is not difficult, it just takes structured practice and time to train your fingers. It will take a few weeks before you begin to feel comfortable. At first, practice by striking the thumb once, then each finger using all three fingers. It is the first picking pattern shown on page 26.

Alternate Base Lines

Each finger hits a treble string and the thumb will alternate between two or more base strings (second example on page 26). A good chord to use is D major. The open string D and A notes serve as the base notes and the thumb will alternate between the two notes. Practicing this will launch the coordination between thumb and fingers.

To Use A Pick Or Not

There are many ways to play the guitar without using a pick. Some people prefer using fingers only and avoiding plastic. Plastic is very useful, but it can take longer to feel comfortable. Strumming can be done without a pick by using the thumb with a back and forth motion but it cannot totally mimic a pick. A pick will have a certain sound. Flat picking will have a different sound than finger picking.

Finger Picking

Finger picking refers to the right hand technique of using combinations of fingers and a thumb to pluck the strings. Flat picking involves the use of a plastic pick. When finger picking each finger sounds a note. When flat picking it takes two fingers to sound a note.

Finger picking can be used in many types of music. Classical guitarists rely on this technique more than most other guitarists. A classical guitarist will develop a complete plectrum style that will rely on three fingers and thumb for chording and combinations, and a two finger interleave technique for scale passages. Two fingers alternate to strike a string so that runs and linear scale passages can be played. The detail placed on classical right hand technique places these guitarists in their own league. Many of these techniques are based on the classical approach.

Some picking patterns will use different combinations of fingers and a thumb. If you play the exercises on page 26, you will work all three fingers and thumb. That will enable you to use whatever combinations you choose. The first picture shows the pinky anchored to control hand position. This can become a crutch. Although it is acceptable, it is important to be able to finger pick with your hand floating without an anchor as in the next picture.

Fingernails

Fingernails are an extremely important component of finger picking. If you can grow strong finger nails you will certainly have an advantage when finger picking. A smooth extended nail combined with the fleshy pad of your finger will give you great control over the exact sound you create. Fingernails will allow each string to ring clearly. If you alter the force, you can change the sound. Since nails are attached to your fingers they offer very good control. You may be able to finger pick well before you master a flat pick.

It was because I have trouble growing strong nails that I learned to use a pick. I have tried to protect mine and I have tried many ways of strengthening them without success. I have had the most success by filing them daily and keeping away from activities that crack them. Regular maintenance and clipping to form a smooth hard edge will help but things like baseball, basketball and frisbee will cause immediate damage to your nails. If you grow nails remember they are for your picking hand only. You should maintain very short fingernails on the fretboard hand. Nails on your fretboard hand can stop you from pressing the string correctly.

You can pick with your fingernails as I do. I still play without a pick and I do not have any problem finger picking. However the sound is not as bright as a person with nails.

Classical Style Or Rest Stroke Style

If you are going to use a classical or finger style approach for scales then try alternating as shown below.
i = index finger, m = second finger and t = third or ring finger. Use two fingers in an alternating fashion.
If you are using the index and second fingers then practice like this:

1. i m i m i m i m i m i
2. m i m i m i m i m i m

If you are using the second and third fingers then try it like this:

1. m t m t m t m t m t m t m
2. t m t m t m t m t m t m t

If you are using the index and third fingers then practice like this:

1. i t i t i t i t i t i t i
2. t i t i t i t i t i t i t

If you play a scale by first ascending then descending and you stop on the same note that you started on, each scale run should end with the finger it started with. If you start on the i, you should finish on the i. Check often until you are sure that you are doing that too. Do not allow yourself to develop bad habits.

Linear Passages

If you do not use a pick when you play, I suggest you play scales using this technique. The reason I suggest this is because you must play scales even if you choose not to use a pick. From this position it is possible to combine full or partial finger picking with scale passages. It can complete the ability to use fingers alone to play even the most demanding parts. Although finger picking will come quickly, this technique usually requires more time to integrate.

Using two fingers in an alternating fashion, strike the same string. First the index finger then the second finger, then the index finger repeats again. You can stop the striking motion by bumping the next lowest string as you follow through, however do not practice this way exclusively. Practice by striking one string without touching any other string. You will not always be able to use a neighboring string. Many passages will require that no other strings be sounded or muted.

You can also place your thumb on the wood as an anchor but it can introduce a dependence. One of the difficulties in this method is the switching of fingers without straying off center into the neighboring strings.

Thin, Medium or Heavy

Different picks have different advantages. Picks come in a variety of shapes and thicknesses ranging from very thin to rigid. For strumming purposes the thin and medium picks will bend slightly. This can facilitate strumming because the pick will gently give way when brushed across the strings. A thick pick will take longer to master because there is no bending. A thick pick will keep the shape and require a greater control to attack the strings and get the desired results. There is a very good reason to use a thick pick however.

 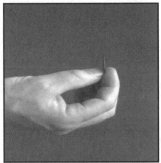

Single note passages (scales) require an exact stroke to repeatedly hit the string correctly. Since a thin or medium pick will bend, it can be harder to hit the string perfectly every time. A thick pick will always be in the same place provided it does not slip in your hand. Play with each kind, so you may understand the differences.

Double Picking

This is a technique for attacking the string from both sides. This technique should be used when practicing scales and creating runs.

When you strike the string from above it is called a downstroke. When you strike the string from beneath the string it is called an upstroke. Speed is built up gradually by combining a downstroke and then an upstroke in a repeating fashion. Just as with the plectrum style, double picking will alternate as you play the scale. If you start with an upstroke you should end with an upstroke. When starting with an downstroke you should end with a downstroke.

It is most common for people to concentrate on starting with a downstroke. Try starting both ways. Sometimes it can be easier to play a scale by starting with an upstroke. Double picking can be practiced by holding down a note or chord and concentrating on the picking motion without moving the fretboard hand. You are isolating the picking motion and several 20 minute sessions can greatly improve your sense of coordination.

String Bending

The high E string is bent to increase the pitch of the note. This note is originally a C#, however by bending the string after striking the string, you can change the note to a D# or an E. That would be an increase of a step and a half. Notice the thumb is out of place, bending strings requires finger strength.

Flat Picking

By introducing the pick, we are increasing the level of difficulty. Now we must hold something while using it to strike one or many strings. It is worth noting that with a pick it takes two fingers to strike one string. Therefore it is not as efficient as finger picking, which takes only one finger to strike a string! There are wide variations on holding a pick and advantages to certain styles. When practicing scales it is good to try holding the pick like this. Expose the pick about 3/16 of an inch at the very end. Wrap the thumb around it so that it does not move when you strike a string. I use a heavy pick so that I have absolute control. Most people use a medium pick but it varies widely.

No matter how you hold the pick at first it will feel awkward. This takes practice to get the relationship between fingers, plastic and strings worked out. Hold down a chord and strike a single note and repeat the striking motion for several minutes. Practice slowly so you get a consistent result. As you strike the string notice if you are breaking your wrist to make the striking motion. The motion to strike the string can be generated from two places, at your elbow and at your wrist. Breaking the wrist to move the pick is the most common way. You can also hold your wrist stiff and generate the motion at your elbow. The elbow generates more power but requires a disciplined approach to execute correctly.

Pick Only

When I play scales I usually close my fingers tightly and allow the pick to stick out about one quarter inch below my fingers. Although it is difficult to see the pick from in front, this is what it looks like. The next shot shows the pick from a slightly different angle with the fingers extended to pick notes.

There are several difficulties you may encounter as you learn. Some typical problems are the pick flying out of your hand as you strum or spinning in your hand as you try to hold it. Usually it takes some time to get the feel of a wedge of plastic. Flat picking chords will definitely help as will playing scales. What you are doing is giving your hands an opportunity to get motions and timing down before it is needed.

Using Pick And Fingers

This is just like finger picking except now you must use the little finger to play the higher treble string and the pick will play the base strings just like the thumb. Because you must hold the pick in two fingers, the little finger must be used to have three fingers available.

The pick can be used only to play the base strings or in combination with strumming, single note passages. You can even use a combination of flat and finger picking.

Start with simple exercises and try to eliminate stray sounds or miscues. The only way to get this is to practice this.

Right Hand Picking Patterns

Picking Patterns

Here are some typical picking patterns shown in tablature. These can be played with a pick and fingers or thumb and fingers. In many cases they can be played with a pick only. Some of the patterns that require you to play two notes at the same time can be tricky for a pick only approach. You may adopt some of these in a slightly different manner to facilitate your flat picking style.

Using Tablature

The exercises below use a variation of tablature. The horizontal lines are the strings, the numbers represent the finger you use to strike the string. The chord is not shown. This is showing right hand only. The first example uses the upper four strings, it starts with the thumb and then uses the index (1) finger, the middle (2) finger and the ring (3) finger to strike the strings. Pick any chord that uses the upper four strings.

Legend

T = Thumb or pick
1 = Index finger
2 = Middle finger
3 = Ring finger

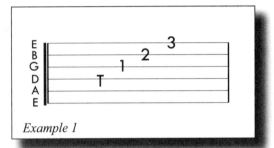

Example 1

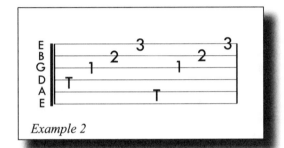

Example 2

Simple Picking Patterns

Use a D chord or a similar chord that uses the upper four strings. D major works well because the tonic or root note is the open string D note (on the fourth string). The first pattern uses only one base note, the open D note. The second one uses an alternating base note. Notice the first three fingers stay the same. This pattern requires that you move the thumb to two positions while keeping the fingers in the same position.

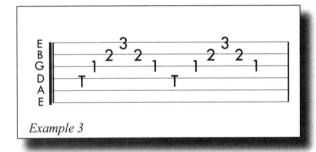

Example 3

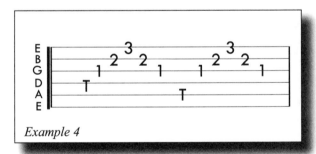

Example 4

Arpeggios

Examples 3 and 4 are standard arpeggios. Use the D chord and the D note as the base. Notice these patterns only require one note at a time. This is a very good exercise to use to help achieve a smooth fluid picking pattern. Use a metronome and hit each note cleanly. Develop a melodic picking ability by using a metronome and finger pick according to the beat. This will take time to develop. The first concern is to play each note cleanly with no glitches between notes. By playing only one chord at first, you can isolate the picking motions without worrying about changing chords. Concentrate on developing coordination with all your fingers. After you are comfortable, introduce new dynamics slowly. Try switching between two chords while picking smoothly. Try to eliminate mistakes between chords. At first your technique will break down in several different ways. After ten or twenty sessions, you should have much greater skills. Try these patterns with the chords in every key. You should now be able to use these patterns to create your own exercises.

Advanced Patterns

The first pattern uses only the thumb and second finger. This is an example of a combination using only two fingers. Try playing the chords G major, C major and D major.

After you get comfortable with the demands on the fingers, you can change base notes to include an alternate base note. These patterns may need to be changed to accommodate the chords you choose. If you play a G chord use the G note for the base note, if you then change to a C chord, the C note would be the logical choice for a base note.

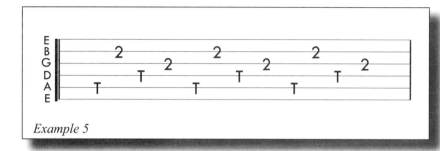

Example 5

Legend

T = Thumb or pick
1 = Index finger
2 = Middle finger
3 = Ring finger

Two Notes At Once

These patterns are helpful for playing two notes at the same time. Notice in exercises 7 and 8, the thumb and third finger hit notes at the same time then the second and index fingers sound notes. It starts with both high and low note and descends to the base note.

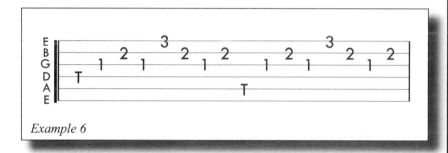

Example 6

Alternating Between Patterns

Eventually you will want to construct or play picking passages in songs. It will become important to be able to jump from one pattern to another. Many times you may need to alter a pattern to accommodate a song passage. It may seem inappropriate to play an entire pattern without modification. Play one pattern and then switch to a new one. Mix them up and add connecting passages to smooth out transitions and add interest. The rhythm of a particular song will no doubt dictate timing that must be accommodated by the picking pattern.

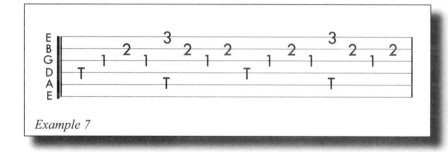

Example 7

Example 8

Start by learning these and other patterns and then adapting them to fit your needs. Artistic skills will begin to emerge as you apply the techniques learned here. Do not be afraid to experiment or play around with these ideas. Not everything will sound good. But trial and error will produce results.

Open String Chords

The Open String Chords

Here is a listing of most of the chords we will use in this book. The chords must be played at the exact fret as shown. For instance if you were to move the B major chord up one fret it would be a C major chord. It does not look like the C major chord we show but it is the same chord. You can move any of these chords to make new chords, for now just be aware that everything is movable both up and down. As we work through the keys you will see these chord forms used to make the chords in that key. The benefit to you is this is about all the chords you need to memorize.

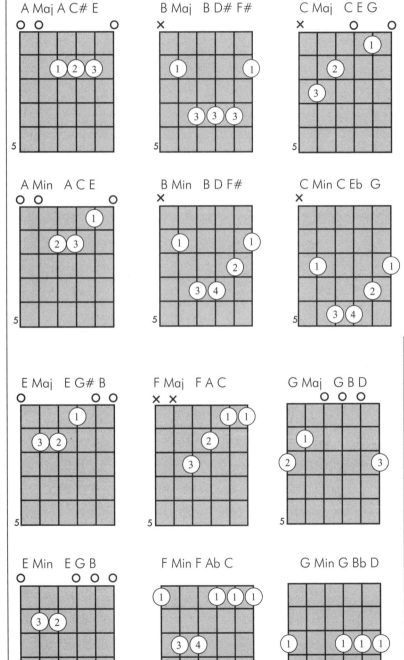

Chord Forms

Look at the B chord again. This is a B chord because it is played at the second and fourth frets. But if you look at the shape of the chord without worrying about frets you are examining the form. Here is this form for reference. This form can become any major chord just by moving it to a new location.

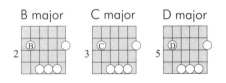

Remember moving one fret up from B, and the chord becomes a C major. Moving it up two frets higher and this form is now a D major. The note in the chords above is the note the chord is built on. Moving to a new note and maintaining the form will change the chord to match the new note. If you move it to the C note it becomes a C chord. Move it to the D note and it becomes a D chord.

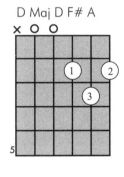
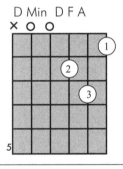

Picture Chords

The Open String Chords

Here are pictures of the chords charts for the previous page. Keep in mind that you can play them differently because there are many different ways to play these chords. We will add more later.

A Major A C# E

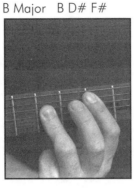

B Major B D# F#

C Major C E G

D Major D F# A

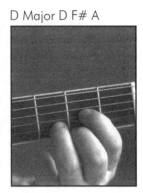

A Minor A C E

B Minor B D F#

C Minor C Eb G

D Minor D F A

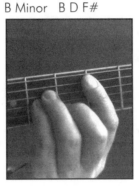

Equating Pictures To Graphics

These pictures will illustrate what it looks like to play the chords. These pictures match the chords on the previous page and make up the chords studied in the diatonic keys.

If you have trouble playing a chord as you go through the book, it may help to look here and make sure you are playing it correctly.

It is important to be able to recognize these chords by looking at charts. Charts are much easier and clearer to use than pictures. The exact placement of fingers can be seen. You must also understand when to barre a chord by looking at a chart.

E Major E G# B

F Major F A C

G Major G B D

E Minor E G B

F Minor F Ab C

G Minor G Bb D

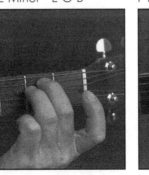

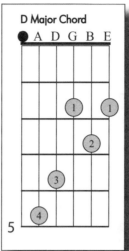

D Major Chord

A D G B E

5

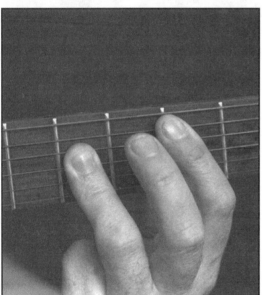

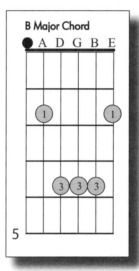

B Major Chord

A D G B E

5

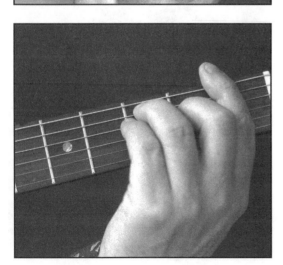

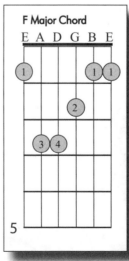

F Major Chord

E A D G B E

5

Barre Chords

These are the true workhorses for the guitar. The group of chords that require some sort of barre is huge and very useful.

A barre chord is any chord that requires a finger to press down more than one string. In the first example the index finger is barring the first three strings. Notice the only strings the index finger must control are the high E and G strings, however the index finger must cross the B string to get to the G string.

The next example I play differently than most people. This chord is usually played with the first and third fingers, however I play it with the first and fourth fingers. I can play it either way but I seem to prefer this way. You may choose to learn it with the first and third fingers. In either case both fingers are barring more than one note, and actually the first finger only needs to control two strings but it must cross five.

Remember that it is not necessary to barre all six strings when you are not using the low E string. Barring strings that you are not playing will force your hand to do more than what is necessary. Over the span of several hours if you are barring more than what you need, you will have to work much harder than if you played only what is necessary. This can cause your finger or hand to fatigue faster. Barre only what you need.

The next example is an F barre chord. The index finger will cross all six strings in order to play the three notes shown on the first fret. Barre chords are easily moved because the barre eliminates the need for open strings. The chord form can be moved with no modification as long as open strings are not used. Notice if you moved the F major chord back one fret, you get an open string E major chord.

Scales

One of the biggest secrets in the musical world seems to be the benefits of incorporating scales into a daily routine. Most people have no idea why anyone would want to do this. If you play scales for one day you may walk away with the notion that they are not for you. If you are a beginner and this is a decision you are mulling over, let me spell it out for you.

If you play scales you will quickly go far beyond a guitarist of similar ability in a very short time. The effect accumulates over time. It is an investment in your future. It will give you benefits in as little as a week after you start to play them, but that is nothing compared to what you will get if you keep playing them.

Scales make you work and the only way you will be able to become a guitar player is through work. Make no mistake about that. If you do not work you will not break through the barriers that are present when you start. If you think you are the exception to work, you are kidding yourself. Someone once told me that if you have potential, it means you have done nothing yet. In a way, there is some truth in that. You must develop your potential. If you think you have hands that can grasp the concepts of the guitar, they must be shown exactly how to play. Until you do that, your hands do not know what to do. It sounds simple but it affects everyone.

Scales are not the only way to become a guitar player, but they are the quickest and surest way of gaining skill. Scales are the foundation of lead guitar. Lead guitar is based on linear streams of notes for lead line construction. If your intention is to become a lead guitarist, scales are the only sure path to get there. If you play scales for several years, you will be capable of screaming leads and melodic statements. You will easily grasp the basics of playing a lead line.

Here then is how you play the simple C scale for the first position.

Playing The C Scale

The notes in this example in order will be E, F, G, A, B, C, D, E, F, G, A, B, C, D, E, F, G. Notice the letters E, A, D, G, B and E above the notes in the circles. These letters are the notes you sound when you play an open string. They are in this scale and must be played.

Play the open E note first. The first note in this example is this E note. Play the E note!
The F note is next. Play the F note.
The G note is next. Play the G note.
Then go to the A string and do the same thing for that string.
Play the open string A note, then the B note, then the C note.
Repeat this for every string.

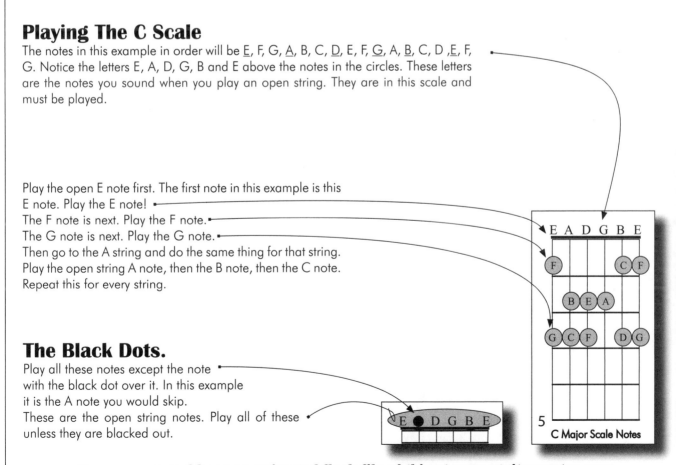

C Major Scale Notes

The Black Dots.

Play all these notes except the note with the black dot over it. In this example it is the A note you would skip.
These are the open string notes. Play all of these unless they are blacked out.

You can see and hear an animated flash file of this at www.eguitarcenter.com

Concentrate On This

You Have Now Read The First Part Of This Book

It has shown you how to hold the instrument and how to create sounds. That is information that will become important as you try to play the next part.

The first section is mostly about reading and thinking. The second part is about playing. The first section supports the second section. It is very important to reread it. As you begin to play the chords and scales, you will generate a bunch of questions. Most of which are discussed in the first section. If you reread that section after you have generated some questions, you will find the answers. After the diatonic keys are presented you will find another section to read. You can read it at any time. I put it there because this is a lot of information to absorb. Much of this will make sense as you play the chords and scales in the next section. The experience you amass will breathe life into the subject matter and in a sense it becomes your own. I call this taking ownership (not an original idea). This approach should stimulate your ability to think freely about music. Free thinking will usually open up new avenues of interest. As you get better it shows up more often and becomes more valuable.

Playing Through The Next Section

Now you know how to hold a guitar and use your hands with the guitar to make sounds. The next section contains chords and scales (among other things) so that you can build up your ability. If you are like most of us, you will question why you are doing this. That is normal.

You practice the fundamentals so when you need to call on your skills, they are in place. In order to get them in place, do this;

Start by reading the text. It contains so much information, you will probably not get all of it right away. Reread it several times over the course of the first year.

Play the scales on each page. You do not have to play them all every day at first. At first you may choose to concentrate on a few keys. This book should last about a year if you use it an hour a day (or longer). Play the scales first because they provide the best exercise. It will strengthen your ability to play the chords.

Play the scales over and over! Scales pay benefits if you use them. Anyone who plays scales will see an immediate and lasting benefit. If you know a song in the key of C, play the scale over the song and see what happens. Experiment!

Then play the chords (at first in order). They will be difficult at first and get easier as you play them. Play them over and over. You should be able to play them cleanly and accurately. It will take time and will get better with each passing day. If you find yourself going off on a tangent with some chords, take the time to explore what you are thinking. Find new combinations that spark interest.
Get into it!

The only way you can learn how to play is by working. Do not be afraid to work. Work holds the answers. Sometimes it is the only way to connect with the guitar.

Every person that learns to play a guitar, does so through work. It is the only way to learn. Combine this work with your choice of songs and you are on your way.

You will not understand everything the first time. The understanding will take shape as you go. Give it time and reread this occasionally. Playing the guitar is a journey, as long as you continue to play, it will never have an end and you will continue to learn new things and apply them to your style. Learning new things will keep you interested.

The Diatonic Keys

Scales And Chords
For The First Position Diatonic Major And Minor Keys

The Diatonic Keys

The diatonic keys are the foundation of music in the western hemisphere. This is the basis for almost all the songs heard on the radio. There are twelve different keys because there are twelve total notes on which you can build a key. All the notes will serve as a keynote for one key. If you stay within the key, all the chords will relate to the key note and cause that note to be the center of the creation.

You can simply play within a key or switch keys as often as you like. The music generated within a key can be quite diverse from song to song. We study keys so we have an understanding of the palette for musical creation. Once we have an understanding in place, we can increase the enjoyment derived from playing the instrument. Learning the diatonic keys is an effective way of becoming familiar with the guitar.

The design is to play the scales in the key, then play the chords in the key, then learn songs in the key. All the time using the finger and flat picking techniques as well as others. Playing songs will show you how other artists use keys. It will give you ideas of how to use them.

The Chords Are Built From The Scale. The first line contains the musical notation for the exact notes for the scale on the next page.

The Second Line. Notice the chords start on the tonic note and climb one note higher for each chord. The chords are created by stacking every other note. This notation describes the chords on the next page.

Understanding The Circle Of Fifths

Understanding the Circle Of Fifths can be very important because it will show you how keys are generated. This will be the guide for key construction. The next key is located five degrees from the one before it.

C Scale

Note	C	D	E	F	G	A	B
Degree	1	2	3	4	5	6	7

The next stop on the circle will be the fifth degree of the key of C which would be G. G will be the next stop. The scales are identical except for one note as you will see.

The Circle Of Fifths

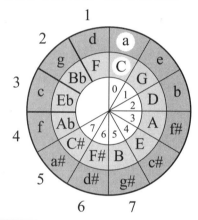

Scales

Everything starts with scales. A key is defined by the notes in the scale. If the notes are C, D, E, F, G, A, and B, you are working in the key of C. It is the scale that determines the key. Remember that every scales starts with the note of the key.

You play a scale by starting on the keynote and proceed alphabetically to the next occurrence of the key note. For instance C, D, E, F, G, A, B and C. Just because the scale starts with the C note does not mean we cannot go lower or higher. We can go backwards like this, C, B, A, G, F, E, D and C. For instance we will start with E and proceed alphabetically. E, F, G, A, B, C, D, E.

For now concentrate on playing the notes of the key of C. The lowest note available is the E string. Start on the low E note and play all the notes in the key of C all the way to the G note on the high E string.

Playing the scale. The notes you will play are E̲, F, G, A̲, B, C, D̲, E, F, G̲, A, B̲, C, D, E̲, F and G. The notes underlined are the open strings. Play them using the open strings. Play the scale this way (ascending) 25 times and then play it descending 25 times. It will seem awkward for a few weeks. You can forget about everything else for a while and just play this. With time this will give you a great feel of the neck.

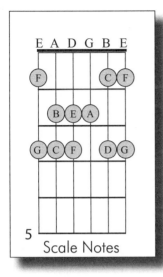

Scale Notes

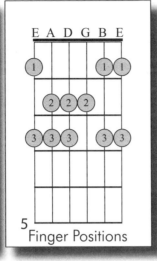

Finger Positions

The Scale of C. Start the scale at the Low E open string. Play the open E, the F and the G note on the low E string. Move to the open A string and play the open A, the B and the C notes. Move to the D string and play the open D and the E and F notes. Move to the G string and play the open G and A notes. Move to the B string and play the open B, the C and the D notes and then move to the high E string and play the open E, the F and the G notes. The first graphic shows the notes, the second graphic shows the finger positions.

Finger Positions
1 = Index Finger
2 = Second Finger
3 = Ring Finger
4 = Pinky

Play the scale notes in order. Play the notes alphabetically starting with the lowest note available! Play these notes. E, F, G, A, B, C, D, E, F, G, A, B, C, D, E, F, and G. The underlined letters are the open string notes. Make sure to play the open strings that have an (O) over the string. Do not play an open string that has an (X) over it.

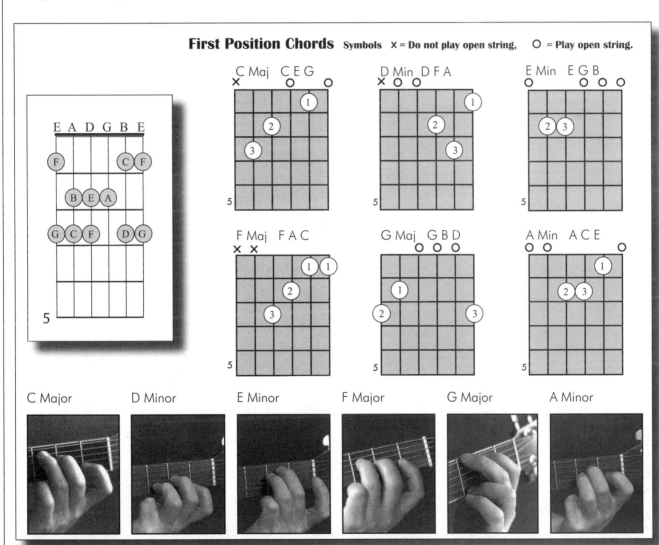

First Position Chords Symbols X = Do not play open string, O = Play open string.

C Major   D Minor   E Minor   F Major   G Major   A Minor

The Key Of G Major

Seventeen Notes In This line. The lowest note in this notation is the E note. The scale climbs two octaves and three notes to end on a G.

The Second Line. Notice the key signature has a sharp on the F note. By looking at the key signature we can tell this is the key of G. G has one sharp, the F # note.

What Makes A Key Unique

Each key is different than all the others. The last or seventh degree of the scale of each key will be sharped (except the key of C).

C Scale   C D E F G A B

　　　　　　 1 2 3 4 5 6 7

G Scale   G A B C D E F#

The F# is the only different note between the two scales.

The Circle Of Fifths

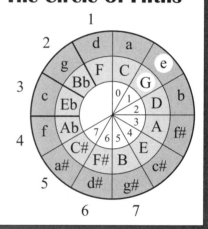

Chords Are Created Using The Scale
You can build a chord on each degree of the scale. The scale contains G, A, B, C, D, E and F#. There are no other notes available. Here is a chart of the key of G and the chords for each degree of the scale. When you play the chords notice you are only playing the notes outlined below.

Degree	Note	Type	Notes Of Chord		
1	G	Major	G	B	D
2	A	Minor	A	C	E
3	B	Minor	B	D	F#
4	C	Major	C	E	G
5	D	Major	D	F#	A
6	E	Minor	E	G	B
7	F#	Diminished	F#	A	C

You will spend a good deal of your time within one key of another. It makes sense to understand how they work. You do not have to memorize this, just be aware this is how keys work.

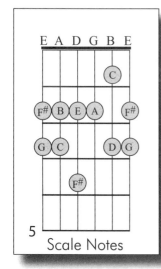

Scale Notes

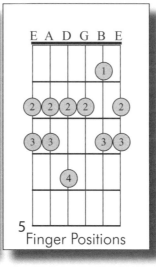

Finger Positions

The Scale of G. The F note is now sharp (F#), other than that it is the same as the C scale. Start the scale at the Low E open string. Play the E open, the F# with the second finger and play the G note with the third finger. Move to the open A string and play the open A, the B and the C notes. Move to the D string and play the open D and the E and F# notes. Play the F# with the fourth finger. Move to the G string and play the open G and A notes. Move to the B string and play the open B, the C and the D notes and then move to the high E string and play the open E, the F# with the second finger and the G with the third finger. The first graphic shows the notes, the second graphic shows the finger positions.

Make sure you play all the notes cleanly. This is very important It should be the highest priority, because it will most likely set up good habits. Sharping the F note is the difference between the G and the C scale. All the notes are the same except the seventh degree of the G scale is now sharp.

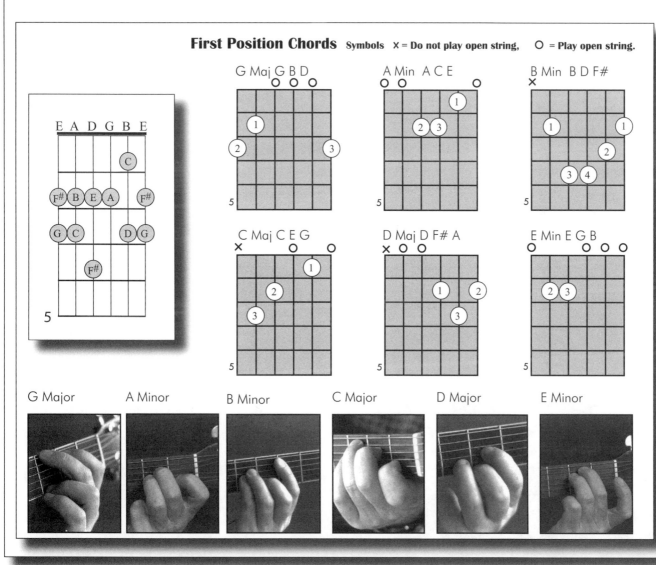

First Position Chords Symbols X = Do not play open string, O = Play open string.

G Major   A Minor   B Minor   C Major   D Major   E Minor

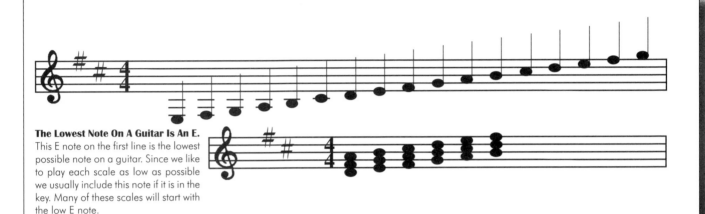

The Lowest Note On A Guitar Is An E.
This E note on the first line is the lowest possible note on a guitar. Since we like to play each scale as low as possible we usually include this note if it is in the key. Many of these scales will start with the low E note.

The Third Key - D Major

D major will carry the sharps of G and add a sharp to the seventh degree of the D scale.

G Scale

G	A	B	C	D	E	F#
1	2	3	4	5	6	7

D Scale

D E F# G A B C#

Do you see that by sharping the C# the D Major scale is now unique.

The Circle Of Fifths

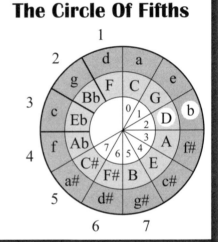

Examining The Structure Of Keys

We have discussed the basic structure of a key by describing how the chords are built in a key. Let look at the different chords. Have you wondered why some are major and some are minor chords?

Tonic. The tonic chord is the chord the key revolves around. D Major is the tonic chord for the key of D Major. This is the central chord in the key. All chords relate to tonic and it is tonic that will bring a piece to rest. This means that you will probably end most songs with the keynote. You will hear this when you run the scale of G. It is the note of G that brings the scale to rest.

The chord type starting with the tonic chord and going through the scale is major, minor, minor, major, major, minor and diminished. After the diminished chord the tonic chord repeats one octave higher.

Degree	1	2	3	4	5	6	7
Type	Major	Minor	Minor	Major	Major	Minor	Diminished
Chord	C Maj	D Min	E Min	F Maj	G Maj	A Min	B Diminished

Notice the 1, 4 and 5 degrees are major chords and the 2, 3 and 6 are minor chords. The chord built on the seventh degree is diminished, this will be explained later. When we talk about a progression that uses the 1, 5 and 4 you will know what chords to play. Referencing degrees makes it easy to switch keys. For instance you can play a 1, 5 and a 4 in the keys of C and D. In the key of D the chords are a D, A and G. It is a simple chord progression, use the chords on the next page to play it.

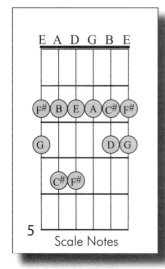

E A D G B E

F# B E A C# F#

G   D G

C# F#

5

Scale Notes

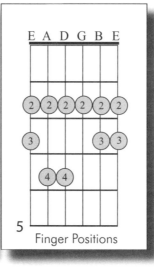

E A D G B E

2 2 2 2 2 2

3   3 3

4 4

5

Finger Positions

The Scale of D. This scale starts with the low E note and proceeds 2 octaves to a G note on the high E string. The sequence is E, F#, G, A, B, C#, D, E, F#, G, A, B, C#, D, E, F#, G. Play it ascending and descending using all the notes available. Play the notes alphabetically. Remember the underlined letters are open string notes.

If you are going to play any notes in the key of D, They must come from this list because these are all the notes in the key. The scale of D uses all the open strings. You may have noticed there are other notes that could be substituted for the open strings. A good example is the B (not shown) note above the A on the G string. As we look at more keys we will begin to use these higher notes.

First Position Chords   Symbols ✗ = Do not play open string,   O = Play open string.

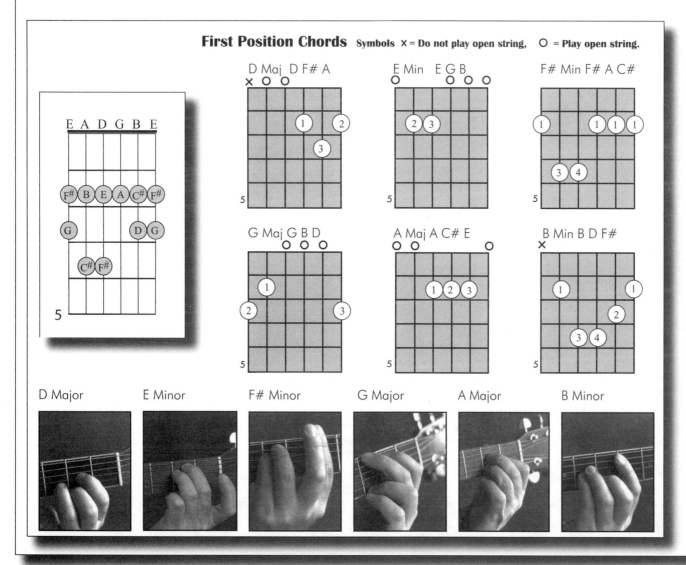

D Major   E Minor   F# Minor   G Major   A Major   B Minor

The First Line. The first line always contains a scale. The scale is usually over two octaves long.

The Second Line. The second line contains the chords built on the notes of the scale. It is important to be able to visualize what chords look like by seeing them on notation.

The Circle Of Fifths

Remember there are twelve notes from E to E (counting all the sharps between notes). Each note represents a key. There are seven notes in each key.

Each key will add a sharp to make it unique.

The Scale of C.	**No sharps**
The Scale of G.	**F#**
The Scale of D.	**F#. C#**
The Scale of A.	**F#, C#, G#**

The Circle Of Fifths

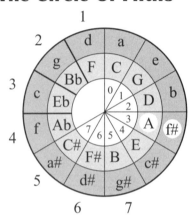

Chord Progressions

Using the key of A as an example, we can play different chord progressions for the key. These progressions will all start with the tonic chord. Start by strumming the chords and listening for the sound of each chord.

Progressions

Degrees	Chord Names
1, 4, 5	A maj, D maj, E maj
1, 5, 4	A maj, E maj, D maj
1, 4, 2, 3, 5	A maj, D maj, B min, C# min, E maj
1, 6, 2, 5, 1	A maj, F# min, B min, E maj, A maj
1, 5, 4, 6, 2, 3	A maj, E maj, D maj, F# min, B min, C# min
1, 2, 3, 4, 5, 6, 7, 1	A maj, B min, C# min, D maj, E maj, F# min, G# dim, A maj. (see page 70).

Notice some progressions are all major, some switch between major and minor and some will play the majors then the minors. There are many reasons why some sound better than others. As we get farther along you will see reasons why some chords relate more strongly to others. There are seven degrees in each key and a chord can be constructed for each degree. Each degree has a personality that will be the same in each key.

Remember to practice the chords in order like the last progression shown. Play them as cleanly as possible. Repeat these progressions 25 times or more. Take your time.

A Major Scale And Chords

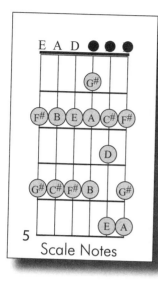

Scale Notes

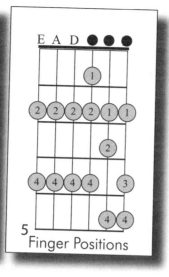

Finger Positions

The Scale of C	No sharps
The Scale of G	F#
The Scale of D	F#, C#
The Scale of A	F#, C#, G#

Notice that when you climb the Circle Of Fifths, you move up five degrees and add a sharp to the previous scale starting with the new note.

By adding a new sharp we are causing this A major scale to be slightly different that the G major scale. This is what give the key a personality.

The scale of A climbs to the A note on the high E string. This is a good scale to hear the sound of tonic. When you hit the A note, the scale seems to be at rest. Play it ascending and descending. A common way to find a key a song is in is to find the note that seems to resolve the song. Run the scale, if it fits, you probably have the right key. There are a lot of little tricks to test for the key signature. As you play these scales, you will develop your ear and learn different tricks for determining what key a song is in.

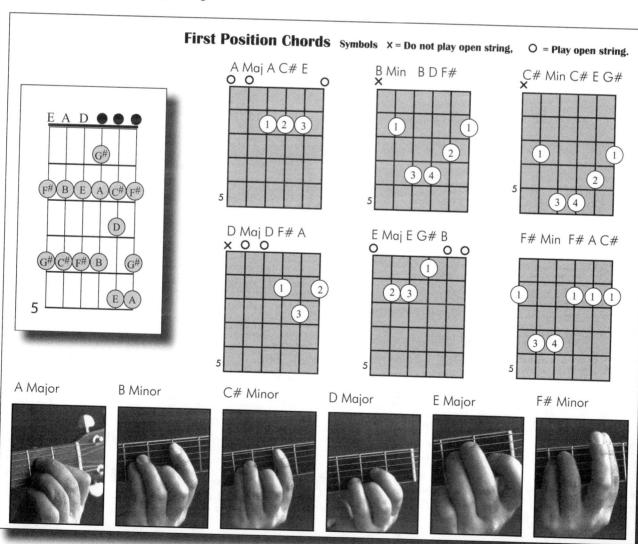

Page 41

The Key Of E Major

The Key Of E Major. Notice there are four sharps in the key signature. The key of E has four sharps, C, D, F and G.

The Second Line. Notice the chords start with the lowest note on the guitar and climb one note at a time. Each chord is created by stacking every other note starting with the note of the key.

The Progression To Other Keys

Someone may say to you play the 1, 5 and 4 chords starting with C and cycling through the circle of fifths from the key of C to the key of E. Here is what you would play.

The Circle Of Fifths

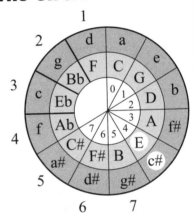

Key	Degrees	Chords
C	1, 5, 4	C maj, G maj, F maj
G	1, 5, 4	G maj, D maj, C maj
D	1, 5, 4	D maj, A maj, G maj
A	1, 5, 4	A maj, E maj, D maj
E	1, 5, 4	E maj, B maj, A maj

Notice. The tonic chord in one example is the fourth chord in the next. Notice the five chord is tonic in the next example as well.

Many chords are interrelated because they share the same notes and they show up in each other's key. Notice that C major and F major are in both keys.

Songs

By now enough chords have been learned so that you should be able to learn to play songs. Take advantage of the printed music you like. Find some easy songs that you can begin to play. The big fake song books will give you many different songs in a simplified arrangement.

You may not know every chord in the songs but you should know and be able to play most of them. Start by strumming the chords and concentrate on playing the chords correctly. It may not sound right at first. You may only be able to play bits and pieces at first. That should change with time.

You are trying to find songs that interest you and will allow you to use some of your new skills. Playing a song that you can hear on a CD or tape will provide a sense of timing for you. It may be hard to keep up with a song or play the rhythm correctly at first.

Remember if you continue to practice the fundamentals, you are steadily building your abilities. In a few months you may be able to come back and play the hard songs correctly. Try five or ten songs and incorporate them into your practice schedule.

Remember scales first, chords second and third you play songs.

E Major Scale And Chords

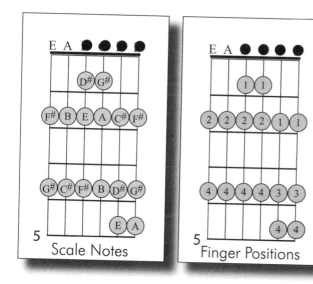

The Scale of C	No sharps
The Scale of G	F#
The Scale of D	F#, C#
The Scale of A	F#, C#, G#
The Scale of E	F#, C#, G#, D#

Notice we are using less of the open strings as we change keys. The key signature above tells you this is the key of E.

This is a very important scale pattern. This is one of the major movable patterns. In this position it is an E major, but if we move it out of the open strings by moving the pattern up one fret it would become a F major. Remember there is one half step between the notes E and F. This is a very good scale to increase your hand strength.

Does Your Hand Hurt? Sooner or later you should try to bear down and play the scales vigorously. Press firmly and increase the level of sound. You should look for opportunities to make your hand ache from playing scales properly.

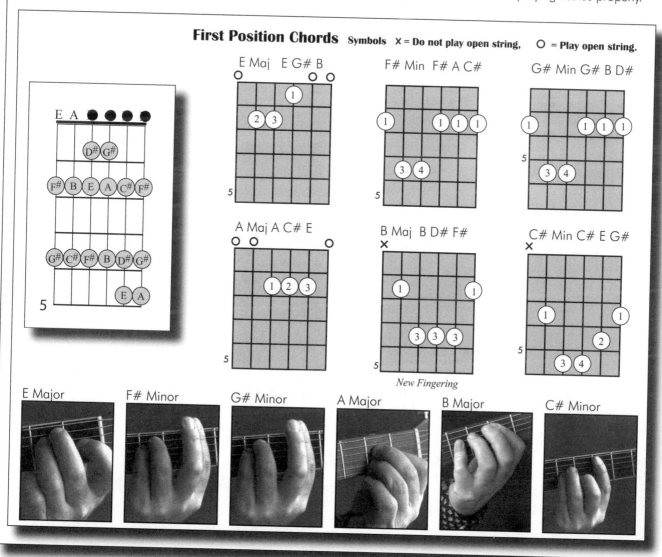

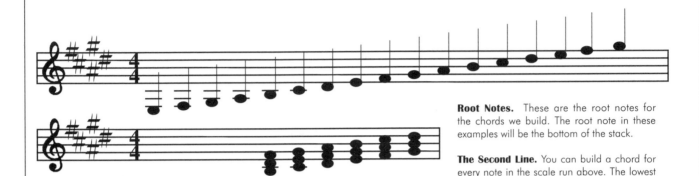

Root Notes. These are the root notes for the chords we build. The root note in these examples will be the bottom of the stack.

The Second Line. You can build a chord for every note in the scale run above. The lowest note here is the root note. The root note of a chord is the tonic note. All these chords have the root as the lowest note.

Relationships Within The Key

Have you noticed the keys are getting more complicated? This key has five sharps and the next will have six.

Notice after C# the circle does not show any more sharps (the inner circle). There are only seven keys but we have to keep changing each new scale.

We actually keep adding sharps but it gets so complicated to see and write so that we describe the next keys by talking about them in terms of flats.

Remember an F# is also a Gb. Every scale can be described in either flats or sharps. We will discuss this but it clearly goes beyond an entry level. Just be aware that you can say it either way.

The Circle Of Fifths

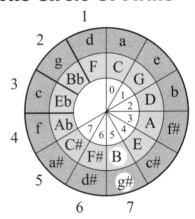

Strumming

Strumming is the basic right or pick hand technique. Every style of music will require you to strum sometime. Strumming is the process of repeatedly striking some or all of the strings in an effort to create a rhythm. Strumming like everything else will get better with time. Practicing with a metronome or click track is very important. At first you will not have command of the technique. A click track will help to get your timing down and learn the feel of following a rhythm.

The purpose of the click track is to help you stay in time. As you develop the ability to strum, you will also develop the ability to strum exactly on time. This will happen as you develop exact muscular motions.

At first do not try to play exotic or unusual rhythms. Just get the feel of strumming and changing chords correctly. Gradually build up strength and speed. Listen for muted or buzzing strings and make sure you are hitting the chords correctly.

When you add a new technique like strumming, it is common to see already learned skills (like forming a chord) take a step backwards. This happens because you are diverting some of your attention to a new element. You may have to think about hitting chords that used to be automatic. It takes time to get everything to work together.

B Major Scales And Chords

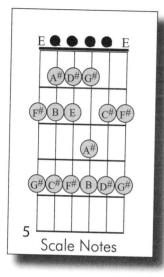

Scale Notes

Finger Positions

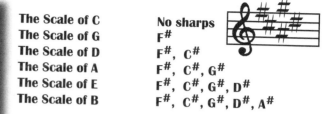

The Scale of C	No sharps
The Scale of G	F#
The Scale of D	F#, C#
The Scale of A	F#, C#, G#
The Scale of E	F#, C#, G#, D#
The Scale of B	F#, C#, G#, D#, A#

Each stop on the Circle of Fifths is five degrees higher than the last and will add a sharp to define the new scale. Each stop is identified by a note that will serve as tonic. That is the keynote and all chords of the key will relate to the tonic chord in a certain way. Each key has seven notes and each key uses notes A through G once. Each key will have a different number of sharps that will give each key a distinct personality. There are twelve keys because there are twelve available notes. Remember there are twelve notes, one for each fret of the guitar starting at fret one and repeating at fret twelve. This is the mechanics of keys.

First Position Chords Symbols X = Do not play open string, O = Play open string.

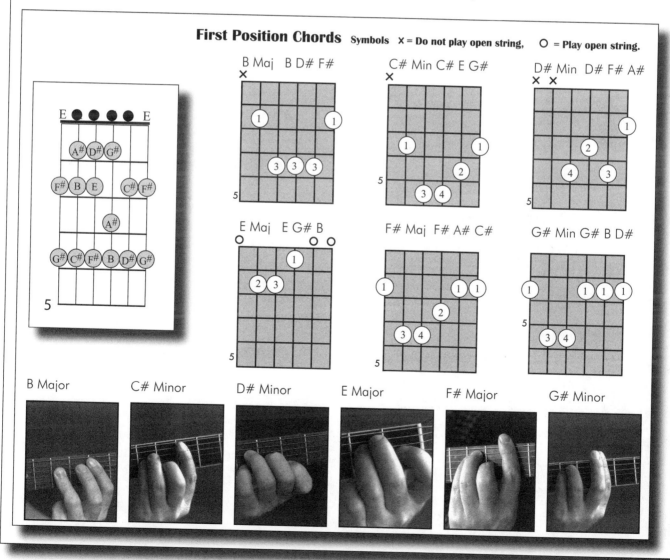

B Major   C# Minor   D# Minor   E Major   F# Major   G# Minor

Root Notes. This musical notation is another way of saying E#, F#, G#, A#, B, C#, D#, E#, F#, G#, A#, B, C#, D#, E#, F#, G#, A#. Check to make sure you get the same answer.

The Second Line. The chords listed on the next page do not always have the root note as the lowest note. You can however build chords just like this music suggests. They are called triads and they have only three notes as shown.

Relationships Within The Key

Here is another way of looking at the shared notes of the key.

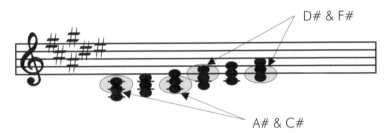

D# & F#

A# & C#

Notice every other chord contains the same two notes. These chords will sound somewhat similar. If you look at this for awhile, you will see several occurrences of each note.

The Circle Of Fifths

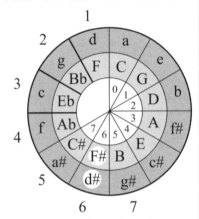

Finger / Flat Picking Chords

How can you play these chords? By playing these chords four different ways, you introduce new elements that must be incorporated to sound correct. Sometimes songs will start with a finger picked passage, then transfer to a strum, and then alternate to a picking passage and back to a strumming passage. By practicing these different techniques you are ready to play them when needed.

1. Strumming the chord. Hold the pick as discussed. Slowly strum a single chord up and down. Establish a steady rhythm and concentrate on sounding all the strings. Eliminate any stray sounds created by inconsistent motions. If you have a metronome or drum machine, turn on a click track for rhythm. Slowly try to switch chords while strumming smoothly.

2. Pluck four notes at once using four different fingers. Play the chord progressions by plucking four notes of each chord at the same time. Use the thumb and the first three fingers, sound every note cleanly. This is a fairly easy technique and should help you to coordinate the movement of each finger. Start by plucking one chord over and over until you start to develop a feel. Then add and switch chords slowly.

3. Finger pick four notes one at a time using four different finger. Do the same as above but play the thumb first, then the index finger, then the middle finger and then the ring finger (modify for use with a pick). At first play them only this way, after a while play them this way and then reverse it. These are arpeggios.

4. Flat pick every note in a chord one note at a time. Start with the lowest note working up to the highest note and descend again. This is called flat picking arpeggios. Play this very slowly and concentrate on the exact motion required. This may take time. You must have a good physical understanding of the picking hand to do this correctly. If you are going to play with a pick, then make this a part of your daily practice schedule. Practice this after you have played scales and are warm. Understanding this will take a few months before you really get the feel. Practice these separately so you isolate the motions.

F# Major Scale And Chords

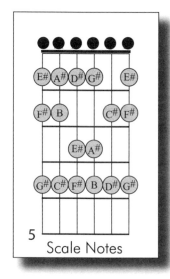

Scale Notes

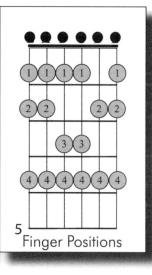

Finger Positions

The Scale of C	No sharps
The Scale of G	F#
The Scale of D	F#, C#
The Scale of A	F#, C#, G#
The Scale of E	F#, C#, G#, D#
The Scale of B	F#, C#, G#, D#, A#
The Scale of F#	F#, C#, G#, D#, A#, E#

Notice that all the notes of the scale are sharp except B. That means that the open strings don't really work for this key because they are not tuned to a sharp. This first position scale moves out of the open strings because of this. The key of F sharp requires that you play a closed scale. This scale does not use open strings. You could substitute the open B note but the B note on the G string works pretty well. Even though this is a beginner scale it is already similar to more advanced scales.

The Key of F#. Remember the key of F? This is just one fret higher. Notice that every note on the first fret is played as an open string in the key of F. We are just moving everything up one fret. All the rules have been maintained. You can skip ahead to page 57 and see the similarities.

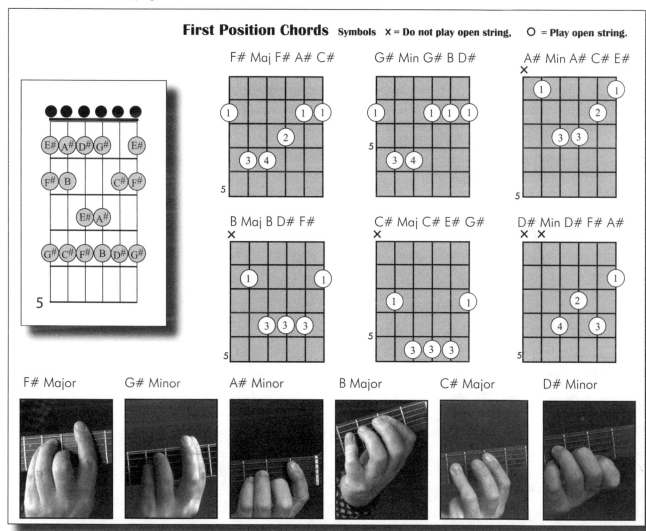

First Position Chords Symbols x = Do not play open string,   O = Play open string.

F# Maj F# A# C#

G# Min G# B D#

A# Min A# C# E#

B Maj B D# F#

C# Maj C# E# G#

D# Min D# F# A#

F# Major   G# Minor   A# Minor   B Major   C# Major   D# Minor

Page 47

Key Signatures. Every key can be expressed in sharps or flats at any time. It is most convenient to change at this key because of several things, one of which is to avoid too many sharps in the signature. You could show the signature with seven sharps or with five flats.

Enharmonic Spellings

Notice the circle changes here. We will reference keys by using flats now. The numbers on the inside of the circle stop at seven because everything is sharped in the key of C#. Think about it, the key of C# is one fret higher than C. If you move a C scale up one fret, what you are doing is sharping every note.

Sharps

Flats

You could use enharmonic spellings for any key. Notice the key of F# has either six sharps or six flats. The key of B could be expressed by using seven flats. For now just be aware of this.

The Circle Of Fifths

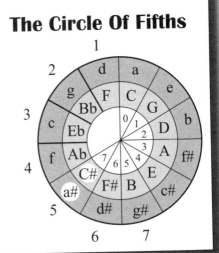

Enharmonic Spellings

So far we have discussed everything in terms of sharps. We have changed each key by adding a sharp to the seventh degree of the scale. Remember we have said a sharp is the same thing as a flat. An F# is the same thing as a Gb. From this point forward we will discuss keys in terms of flats instead of sharps. We will do so because it is easier to talk about flats than double sharps. On a musical staff it is much easier to describe this key in terms of flats. This is an advanced concept, we are discussing it here because some people will wonder about it.

Remember there are at least two names for every chord. We could call a F# a Gb if we wanted, but it gets harder to say F## instead of G.

Think about this if you start at an F and double sharp it (##) you get to G. Remember every time you add a sharp you move up one fret. Moving an F once makes it an F#, moving it again makes it a G. Double sharps will become important in the next key because we are going to use one to make the scale.

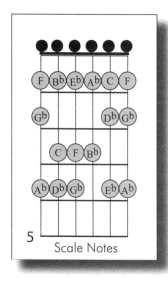

Scale Notes

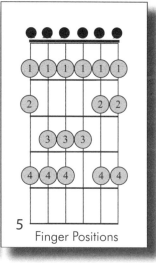

Finger Positions

The Scale of C	No sharps
The Scale of G	F#
The Scale of D	F#, C#
The Scale of A	F#, C#, G#
The Scale of E	F#, C#, G#, D#
The Scale of B	F#, C#, G#, D#, A#
The Scale of F#	F#, C#, G#, D#, A#, E#
The Scale of C#	F#, C#, G#, D#, A#, E#, B#

In the key of C# all notes are sharped. You can still use sharps or flats to describe a key. Remember a C# is also a Db. The notes are the same but they are described as flat.

Enharmonic Spelling

C# D# E# F# G# A# B#
Db Eb F Gb Ab Bb C

Notice the notes are the same, they are just spelled differently. Look at the fretboard and make sure you see a C# is also a Db. We are going to start referring to keys by their flat names because it is easier than dealing with more and more sharps. Check all the notes to make sure you can spell them either way correctly. **Notice the Flat spelling is used in the scale above and the sharped spelling is used below. It is the same scale.**

First Position Chords Symbols ✗ = Do not play open string, O = Play open string.

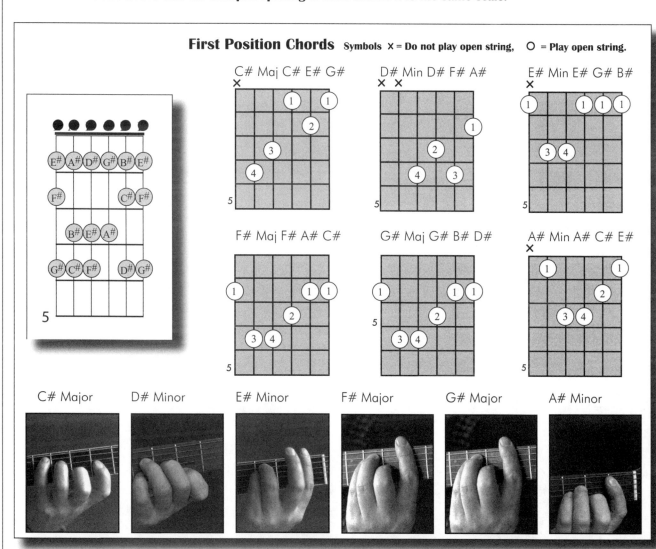

C# Major   D# Minor   E# Minor   F# Major   G# Major   A# Minor

The First Line. The relative minor is here in this scale too. The dashed line shows the same notes make up the relative minor.

The Second Line. The chords for the relative minor are the same as the related major. Just start at the F chord and number it one, then proceed up the scale. Remember the G diminished chord is omitted in this example.

Moving Through Keys

We will change the next key by taking away one flat. This is actually the same thing as adding a sharp to a key as we have done previously.

The key of Eb will have only three flats. The key of Bb will have only two flats. We are three quarters around the circle and you may see that if we keep giving away flats with every new key, we will have no flats left after the key of F major.

Remember the key of C has no sharps or flats. At the key of C we will have completed one trip around the circle.

The Circle Of Fifths

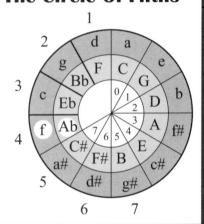

Everything On A Guitar Is Movable

I have said that everything is movable. The key of A and Ab are good examples of this. If you start with an A note and you move it back one fret it will be an Ab. Any chord in the key of A can be moved one fret back and become the same chord only in the key of Ab. In fact five of the chords in this key are actually the chords for the key of A, but they have been moved back one fret.

Another element that can be moved is the scale. Notice that the Ab scale is the A scale only moved back one fret. This will become a very important concept later.

For now make sure that you understand it at the level discussed here. Remember everything is movable! Does this imply there may be shortcuts to learning?

Yes, more than you might think!

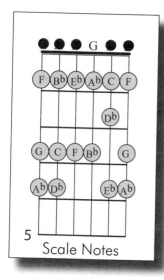

Scale Notes

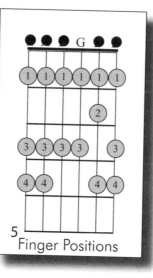

Finger Positions

The Scale of C	No sharps
The Scale of G	F#
The Scale of D	F#, C#
The Scale of A	F#, C#, G#
The Scale of E	F#, C#, G#, D#
The Scale of B	F#, C#, G#, D#, A#
The Scale of F#	F#, C#, G#, D#, A#, E#
The Scale of C#	F#, C#, G#, D#, A#, E#, B#
The Scale of G#	F##, C#, G#, D#, A#, E#, B#

We have added another sharp to the F#. Remember we can describe the key by either flats or sharps. Here is the enharmonic spelling. Notice by adding another sharp we also take away a flat. When we added a second sharp to F#

Example: Enharmonic Spelling

G# A# B# C# D# E# F##

A♭ B♭ C D♭ E♭ F G

to make F## it is actually a G. An F## is another way of saying G.

The Key of Ab/G#. Ab is one fret below A, so expect to see some similarities between the two keys. Repetition is a big part of music. If you can take advantage of it you can drastically reduce what must be memorized.

First Position Chords Symbols X = Do not play open string, O = Play open string.

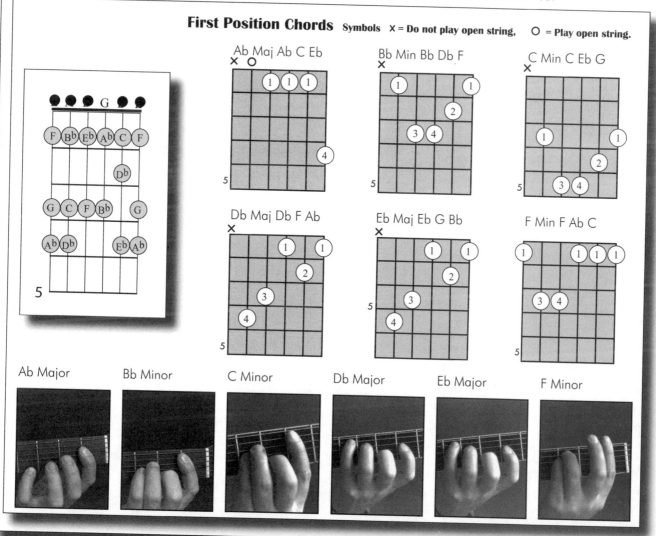

Ab Maj Ab C Eb

Bb Min Bb Db F

C Min C Eb G

Db Maj Db F Ab

Eb Maj Eb G Bb

F Min F Ab C

Ab Major   Bb Minor   C Minor   Db Major   Eb Major   F Minor

The First Line. Notice the lowest note available is the F because the E is flat and the lowest note on the guitar is an E.

The Second Line. We have shown an Eb chord even though the Eb note as shown here is not available. We can however play an Eb chord, we just have to play the Eb note one octave higher.

The Circle Is Continuous

Do you see that by moving five degrees at a time we can travel around the circle and arrive at the key of C without any break down. The keys are symmetrical and very tightly integrated.

Many times a song will start out in one key and switch to another. The progressions often stay the same but the chords used are in the new key. Keys are the basis for most of what we hear and play!

The Circle Of Fifths

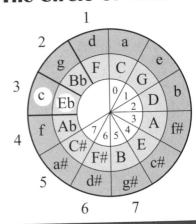

Favorite Keys

Everyone has their favorite keys. For many of us they are the first few on the circle. The keys of C, D, G, A and E are very common in rock and pop. Advanced music groups like country and jazz will use any key and will certainly insert more chord varieties than we have discussed.

These types of music will use this same information in such a way that you may not recognize it. Subtle twists and additions to the basic structure of a song can drastically alter the music. They are built on a foundation of keys and all forms of music will use these basic rules.

You will most likely not play in every key for awhile. But practicing in each key will not only make you familiar with each one but you will play chords in the neighboring keys as well. It will help your total sense of music. It's like breaking down your walls from both sides of the barrier. This is a long term learning experience. It will pay big dividends even after several years.

E♭ Major Scale And Chords

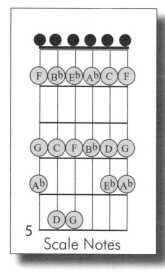

Scale Notes

Finger Positions

Example: Enharmonic Spelling

D♯ E♯ F♯♯ G♯ A♯ B♯ C♯♯
E♭ F G A♭ B♭ C D

The Scale of C	No sharps
The Scale of G	F♯
The Scale of D	F♯, C♯
The Scale of A	F♯, C♯, G♯
The Scale of E	F♯, C♯, G♯, D♯
The Scale of B	F♯, C♯, G♯, D♯, A♯
The Scale of F#	F♯, C♯, G♯, D♯, A♯, E♯
The Scale of C#	F♯, C♯, G♯, D♯, A♯, E♯, B♯
The Scale of G#	F♯♯, C♯, G♯, D♯, A♯, E♯, B♯
The Scale of D#	F♯♯, C♯♯, G♯, D♯, A♯, E♯, B♯

What separates this key from the previous? We have placed another sharp on the seventh degree of the D♯ scale. That note is a C♯♯ now. Notice that every note is used once in a scale. Even though a C♯♯ is a D, we do not call it a D because there is already a D♯. This is a hard concept to grasp. Look at the notes on the graphic as you think about it.

The Key of Eb/D♯. Since these last few keys do not use some open strings it becomes more difficult to play the chords. Open strings are now played by pressing down notes with your fingers.

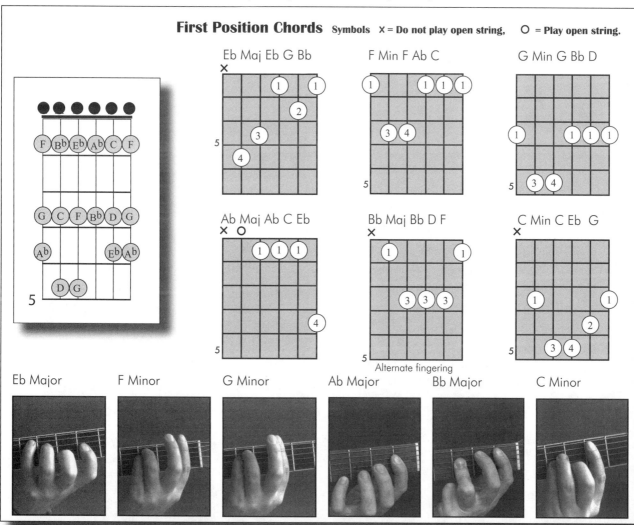

First Position Chords Symbols **x** = Do not play open string, **O** = Play open string.

Eb Maj Eb G Bb

F Min F Ab C

G Min G Bb D

Ab Maj Ab C Eb

Bb Maj Bb D F
Alternate fingering

C Min C Eb G

Eb Major F Minor G Minor Ab Major Bb Major C Minor

The Key Of B♭ /A# Major

The First Line. Linear scales contain every note in the key. These are single note scales. You could think of the chords below as three note scales. That is what they are.

The Second Line. Notice that when we build chords we are using all the notes. In the first two chords here we have used six different notes and the first six degrees of the scale.

The Circle Uses Every Note Available

When we get to F, we will have used every note possible as a keynote. Here is an example of thinking chromatically or in five degree jumps. Between E and E there are only twelve notes as shown below.

Chromatically 1 2 3 4 5 6 7 8 9 10 11 12 1
              E, F, F#, G, G#, A, A#, B, C, C#, D, D#, E
Fifths   5,12, 7, 2, 9, 4, 11, 6, 1, 8, 3, 10, 1

Notice that every note is used. It gets confusing to see that you use every key when you are jumping five degrees at a time.

The Circle Of Fifths

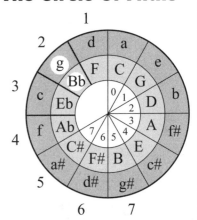

Closed String Scales

This scale is more difficult than any other so far. Some of the others have been closed scales but none have required a five fret stretch. Notice this scale requires you to play three notes over five frets for the lowest three strings. You may have trouble sounding all these notes correctly at first. You must develop strength to hold down the notes of this scale. This is complicated by the fact that this fingering is so close to the nut. The strings are harder to press down here. As you move towards the middle of the fretboard the strings are easier to press down.

This scale pattern is used extensively by intermediate and advanced guitarists. It covers a lot of ground and is quite versatile in every key. Learn it well at this position and practice until you can play it without buzzing or muting any strings. This should make your hand hurt.

We have lost the opportunity to use any open strings with this and the last few keys.

B♭ Major Scale And Chords

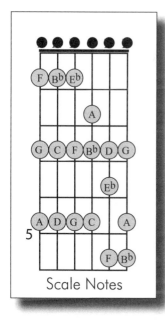

Scale Notes

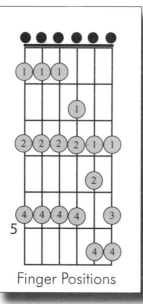

Finger Positions

The Scale of C	No sharps
The Scale of G	F#
The Scale of D	F#, C#
The Scale of A	F#, C#, G#
The Scale of E	F#, C#, G#, D#
The Scale of B	F#, C#, G#, D#, A#
The Scale of F#	F#, C#, G#, D#, A#, E#
The Scale of C#	F#, C#, G#, D#, A#, E#, B#
The Scale of G#	F##, C#, G#, D#, A#, E#, B#
The Scale of D#	F##, C##, G#, D#, A#, E#, B#
The Scale of A#	F##, C##, G##, D#, A#, E#, B#

Even though we will really call these keys by the flatted spelling it is important to see the difference between keys by using sharps. Each key is different because a note was sharped. This has changed the sound of the key and the music created in the key. This is the cause for the personality of each key.

Example: Enharmonic Spelling

A# B# C## D# E# F## G##
Bb C D Eb F G A

First Position Chords

Symbols X = Do not play open string, O = Play open string.

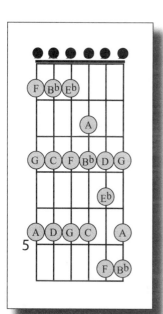

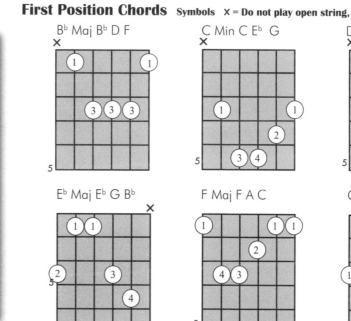

B♭ Maj B♭ D F

C Min C E♭ G

D Min D F A

E♭ Maj E♭ G B♭

F Maj F A C

G Min G B♭ D

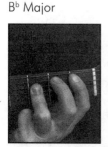

B♭ Major

C Minor

D Minor

E♭ Major

F Major

G Minor

The First Line. This is very close to C major. In fact the only difference is the Bb in the key of F. The fifth degree of F is C.

The Second Line. You should now be able to recognize these chord forms are triads. If you continue using Uncle Tim's Book Of Chords, you will see these same chords in three different arrangements. By changing the arrangement of notes you are changing the inversion.

These Are The Twelve Diatonic (Western) Keys

Most every song will be in one of these keys. Each song will be composed of chords, single note passages and variations in between.

You are familiar with all the keys, now it is a matter of knowing them better. The circle represents nearly the whole world of western music. You have your hands around it, now you put it to work. Most of the time we have discussed the major keys but we could have talked in terms of the minor keys. We have covered them all.

The Circle Of Fifths

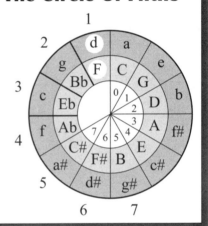

Once Around The Circle

The key of F will conclude one trip around the circle of fifths. We have started with the key of C and jumped ahead five degrees to make each new key. We have repeated that until we arrive here. As you may already see we are going to arrive at C if we go ahead five degrees. In terms of sharps the key of F has F##, C##, G##, D##, A#, E#, B#. The key of C will add a sharp to the A so that it looks like this, F##, C##, G##, D##, A##, E#, B#. If you take the time to examine the enharmonic spelling you will see this translates into C, D, E, F, G, A and B! The circle is integrated very tightly.

Again for now just be aware this is happening. It will become more apparent as you think about it. It is more important to know that we have traveled around the circle and everything fits nicely together. Also notice we are using the open strings more now. Since the key of F contains only one flat (Bb), we are able to use the open strings all except the B.

F Major Scale And Chords

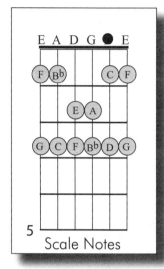

Scale Notes

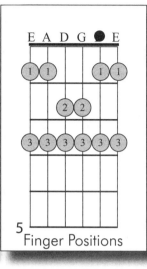

Finger Positions

The Scale of C	No sharps
The Scale of G	F#
The Scale of D	F#, C#
The Scale of A	F#, C#, G#
The Scale of E	F#, C#, G#, D#
The Scale of B	F#, C#, G#, D#, A#
The Scale of F#	F#, C#, G#, D#, A#, E#
The Scale of C#	F#, C#, G#, D#, A#, E#, B#
The Scale of G#	F##, C#, G#, D#, A#, E#, B#
The Scale of D#	F##, C##, G#, D#, A#, E#, B#
The Scale of A#	F##, C##, G##, D#, A#, E#, B#
The F Scale	F##, C##, G##, D##, A#, E#, B#

This is the last stop on the Circle Of Fifths. The only difference between F and C is the Bb in F major. When we started to talk in terms of flats we started taking away flats when we made new keys. Now at F major we have only one flat left a Bb. Could we describe the key of C by adding another sharp? Yes.

The C Scale F##, C##, G##, D##, A##, E#, B#
G, D, A, E, B, F, C

They are not in order but these are the notes of C major.

Enharmonic Spelling

E#	F##	G##	A#	B#	C##	D##
F	G	A	Bb	C	D	E

First Position Chords Symbols x = Do not play open string, O = Play open string.

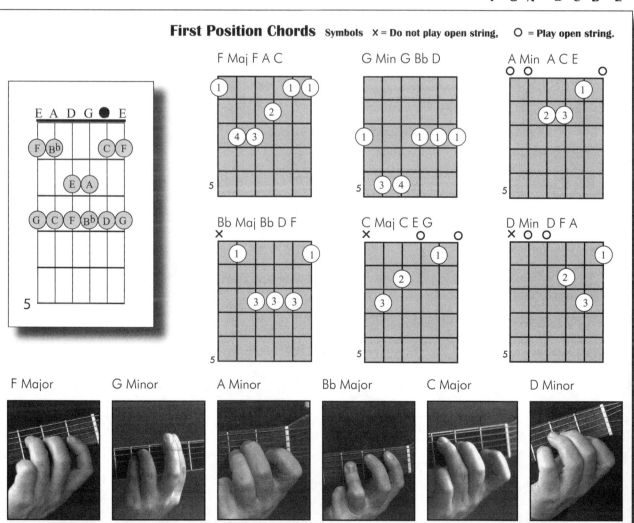

F Maj F A C   G Min G Bb D   A Min A C E

Bb Maj Bb D F   C Maj C E G   D Min D F A

F Major   G Minor   A Minor   Bb Major   C Major   D Minor

The Notes Of The Treble Clef and The Note of C

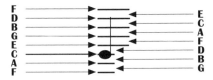

The Notes of The Treble Clef

The Treble Clef with The Note of C

Components Of The Treble Clef and The Note of C

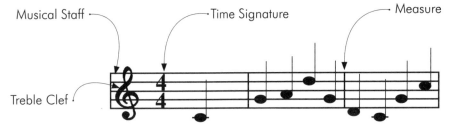

Types Of Notes

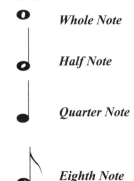

Whole Note

Half Note

Quarter Note

Eighth Note

Note Values
These are common notes you will see when you read musical notation. The difference is the length of time the note is sounded.

A whole note is twice as long as a half note and four times as long as a quarter note. If a whole note is one beat per measure, an eighth note is eight beats per measure. Reading music is a study unto itself, this is an introduction to terms.

How Much Do You Need?

We are interested in looking at chords and scales being constructed. Each key will present the notation of the chords and scales under discussion.

Be aware there is much more to know.

Very often the first note encountered in a piece of music is the keynote. When you see a note or a chord such as the C here it often sets the tone for the piece.

Reading Music

Reading music requires you to be familiar with these symbols. Reading sheet music is an in-depth skill that is learned over time. The musical notation presented in this book is meant to teach you what chords and scales look like when you see them notated. While some song books will require you to learn songs by actually reading the notes and constructing it on a guitar. Most song books will provide chord charts for guitar and notation for piano. Starting out with chord charts is easier and will allow you to play almost immediately. While most guitarists do not sight read, many do read some notation. It is a great skill to have.

If you are going to develop your ability at reading music, start by picking easy songs. There are books that will fully explain notation including the many symbols that will tell you how to proceed. This in depth information is beyond the scope of this book.

Improvisation

Improvisation

One of the biggest benefits from studying chords and scales is the ability to improvise. If you have memorized the six chords and scale for any key, you are qualified to begin. Usually improvisation takes two or more people. Typically they start with a few chords in a key. An improv in the key of G might look like this. A chord progression of G, D, C, G, played fairly slowly to start. The second guitarist would create a lead line from the scale of G. A lead line is different than the scale in that you are selecting notes from the scale. You are not necessarily using all the notes in the scale and you are not usually playing them in order. Do not worry about this too much in the beginning.

If the chords form a nice progression and the lead line flows over the chords, a nice improvisation might develop. The sky is the limit and the only common things most songs share is that they are structured around a key. The more you practice chords and scales the better developed your improvisational abilities will be. With time it is shocking what can happen. This can be one of the most expressive forms of music you will ever play. Remember that we are trying to get a feel for this. It will not all sound good. Experimentation is a must. Do not take it too seriously and you will get better results. When you improvise you are not allowed to worry. Think about the choices for construction and try to have fun.

G Maj G B D

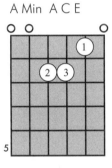

A Min A C E

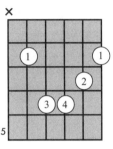

B Min B D F#

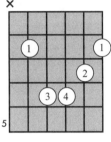

C Maj C E G

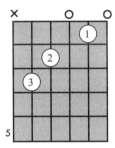

D Maj D F# A

E Min E G B

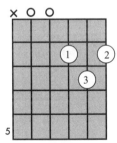

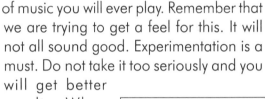

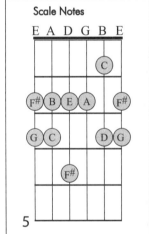

Scale Notes

Theory, I Hate Theory

At the mere mention of the word theory, many people go away. Why would I want to learn theory? This is why. Playing guitar is fun and theory helps you to play much better. **If you learn to play a lead line over some chords, you will like it!** The problem is most people don't know how to do it or they think it is beyond them. The truth is, it's easy and fun.

Theory is the set of rules that govern music. You do not need to know everything, just the basics of how things work and flow. Learning it now will make it available to you as you grow. If you are trying to become a song writer, it will give you guidelines to construct songs. If you are trying to figure out songs, this will provide the palette. Many things about music will not make sense unless you play, think and give it time. Learning theory is like taking off the blinders and seeing the world for the first time. When you recognize how things you already know fit in, it will blow you away! That will happen because you will see the benefits and understand the power available. Reading this section several times is a very good idea. Learning this will help your mind understand what you have been teaching your fingers.

What Do We Need?

There are many different topics that we can study using theory! For instance we could study the micro tones between common notes. We can study exotic scales in an effort to produce feelings. But what we need to know right now is simple.

The theory we will use revolves around the basic and useful information which will surely be evident in the songs most of us play. All western music will revolve around the theoretical concepts available here. The biggest reason we focus on this is because it will always be useful. Theory is simply an exploration of the concepts and rules that affect sound. Here then are the basics which every new guitarist should know. By now you have heard most of this at least once.

Notes

There are twelve notes available on the guitar. This is determined by the spacing of the frets. The twelve notes are A, A#, B, C, C#, D, D#, E, F, F#, G and G#. Notice there are sharps between some notes and not others. As you know there are no notes between B and C. If you sharp the B and make a B#, it is actually a C. You may call it a B# if you want, but it is a C.

Look At The Guitar Fretboard And Notice Two Things.

First, the same twelve notes will repeat on every string every twelve frets. One note per fret, twelve frets until it repeats (in order).

Second, notice there are no spaces between B and C and E and F. Sharp or flat the note and they become the note before or after it. Sharping a note means to raise it one half step or one fret. Flatting a note means to lower it one half step or one fret. Every fret represents a half step, two frets is a whole step.

Keys

Diatonic keys are constructed by using the twelve notes to create twelve keys that will contain seven notes in every key. All keys will have the same spaces between notes.

Every key has seven notes and they are spaced in a very exact pattern. For instance the key of C has seven notes, they are C, D, E, F, G, A and B. It does not matter what order you use, if you use these seven notes you are in the key of C. The key of G has seven notes they are G, A, B, C, D, E and F#. If you are in the key of C and you change the F to an F# you alter the key to a G. Every key will be unique and every key will also adhere to this rule. Starting with the keynote and proceeding up the scale alphabetically the spacing of notes is whole step, whole step, half step, whole step, whole step, whole step, half step. Over the next few pages you will see the key of C, G and D diagramed to show you that it does follow this rule.

Each Scale Has Seven Notes

Each scale has seven notes and therefore seven positions used to develop chords. The different positions can be called degrees and have numbers. For instance the key of C has seven notes, C, D, E, F, G, A and B. It also has seven degrees, they are 1, 2, 3, 4, 5, 6 and 7. You could compare the two expressions with this example.

Note	C	D	E	F	G	A	B
Degree	1	2	3	4	5	6	7

The Chromatic Pattern

E A D G B E

F	A#	D#	G#	C	F
F#	B	E	A	C#	F#
G	C	F	A#	D	G
G#	C#	F#	B	D#	G#
A	D	G	C	E	A
5
A#	D#	G#	C#	F	A#
B	E	A	D	F#	B
7
C	F	A#	D#	G	C
C#	F#	B	E	G#	C#
D	G	C	F	A	D
10
D#	G#	C#	F#	A#	D#
E	A	D	G	B	E
12

So What?

These different degrees are the things we can use to build songs in each key. In other words if you are learning a song in the key of C you can use chords for the key of C. If you understand the key that a song is in, you are in a much better position to learn and master the song quickly. You can do this quickly, because you are already familiar with the key. When you see something time and time again you get better at recognizing it and using it. Eventually you will see a song and play it well the very first time. That happens because you have practiced the chords and can ask your hands to do things correctly the first or second time. That skill will only come with time spent on the fretboard. You must be very familiar with the movement of your hands to produce music. Since this will take some major time to really learn, it makes sense to understand what it is that is worthy of such huge amounts of your time.

Note	C	D	E	F	G	A	B
Degree	1	2	3	4	5	6	7
Chord type	Maj	min	min	maj	maj	min	dim

Each degree is either a major chord, a minor chord or a diminished chord. The example above shows you the first, fourth and fifth chords are always major. The second, third and sixth chords are minor, and the seventh chord is diminished.

Why?

It is this way because the spacing of notes in each key is the same. A chord can either be major, minor or diminished. You may have seen other kinds like an augmented chord but that is not considered with these keys and scales. If you study this, you will understand augmented chords when they are presented in Uncle Tim's Book Of Chords.

The Key Of C

Here is the key of C. Compare it to the chromatic scale and notice the key of C uses only seven notes and has no sharps or flats. Notice that each string flows alphabetically and climbs the scale. Remember the sharps/flats are present, we are skipping the notes because they are not in the key. The fretboard is shown for twelve frets, however we are going to discuss only the first five frets or so. I call this the first position. With five frets you can play one whole example of each chord for each key (actually there is more than one way).

If you go above the fifth or sixth fret you travel into the next position. If you are interested in working here, you still use the scale and chords for the key. We are not going to do much at the second position now. We are going to concentrate in the first position. If you understand how the first position works, going up the fretboard will actually be fairly easy. The hard part is learning the rules. After we see how the rules work, we begin to really understand the guitar. Once the first position is learned, the rest will fall right into place.

Notice

The graphic only contains the notes in the key of C.

Starting at the note of C and climbing any string the spacing will always be whole step, whole step, half step, whole step, whole step, whole step, half step. Look now and make sure you see this for every string.

Then notice that all notes in the key occur on every string and they repeat every twelve frets. The only notes you are seeing are the notes for the key of C. You are seeing several examples of each note, but they are only the notes in the key of C. We repeat this several times because it is really important and much of what will follow is based on it. Over the next several pages we will look at this in detail. **Make sure you understand this as we go through it!**

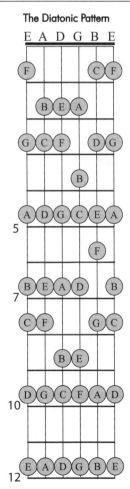

The Diatonic Pattern

Intervals And The Circle Of Fifths

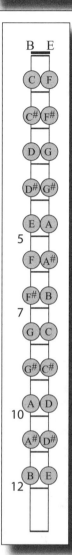

The Twelve Chromatic Notes

All available notes for construction are present in the chromatic scale. Every fret contains a note and every note is in the chromatic scale. Do you see that if you start at C and go up the string until you arrive at C again you will go twelve frets and play twelve notes. Each note is a keynote on the circle of fifths. When we play or create music it is almost always in one of these diatonic keys.

Each note has a scale that starts with that note and adheres to the spacing of whole step, whole step, half step, whole step, whole step, whole step, half step. Notice that C, D, E, F, G, A, and B already conforms to this rule. There are no sharps or flats and this denotes the key of C. This is the first position on the circle of fifths. Every other scale will have at least one sharp.

Notes And Distances Between Notes

The graphic on the right shows the key of C for the highest two strings of the guitar. All keys shall proceed with the following spacing for creating scales. Whole step, whole step, half step, whole step, whole step, whole step, half step. Look at the C note on the graphic. The distance between C and D is a whole step. The distance is two frets. Between E and F is a half step. There are no frets between the E and F notes. They are one fret apart.

Notice that starting with the note of C and progressing up the string the spacing is whole step, whole step, half step, whole step, whole step, whole step, half step. Every key will be built using this rule.

Notice that C repeats on the same string twelve frets higher. Remember there are notes at each fret. Since there are twelve frets before C repeats, there are twelve notes possible. Each note has a place on the circle of fifths. Each note represents a key. Each key will use the same spacing of whole steps and half steps but each key will be unique.

The Circle

Everything fits together in a circular fashion. There are twelve notes and twelve keys. There are twelve positions on the circle of fifths. The circle shows the path for key construction using the twelve notes. For now just notice how everything fits together.

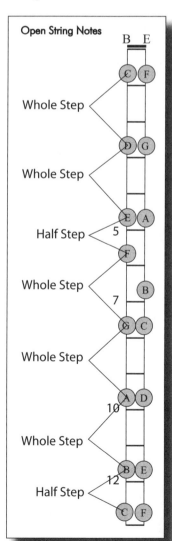

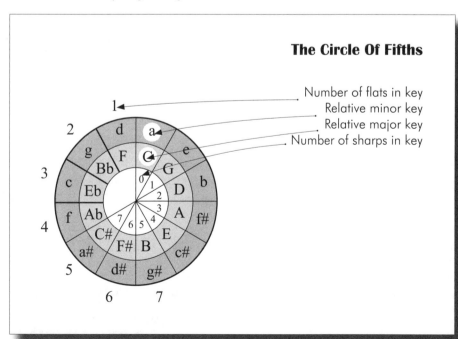

Page 62

Key Construction Using The Scale

Below are three graphics of three different keys. The key of C, the key of G and the key of D. The key of C has no sharps and the key of G is identical except for the F#. The key of D has two sharps the F# and C#. All keys contain seven notes A through G. Each key will add a sharp and carry over the sharps of the previous keys. The next key will always be five degrees above the previous key. Notice G is five degrees above C and D is five degrees above G. The Circle Of Fifths diagram is an easy way to visualize the circular nature of key construction.

Much of the reason we are discussing this information is just to get it in your head. It does not have to be totally clear yet. As you grow in your ability, this information will take shape. For now, get familiar with the concepts by seeing them displayed in the pictures.

What Makes A Key Unique?

Every key will use all seven notes but contain a unique group of sharps. No two keys contain the same sharps or flats.

What Do Keys Have In Common?

The spacing. Notice the progression of whole steps and half steps is the same no matter what example you use. All keys starting with the key note will have intervals that progress as shown. The intervals will always be whole step, whole step, half step, whole step, whole step, whole step, half step. It is the addition of sharps that allows this spacing to occur for all keys.

Look at any key in any example and it will always contain the same whole steps and half steps as described here.

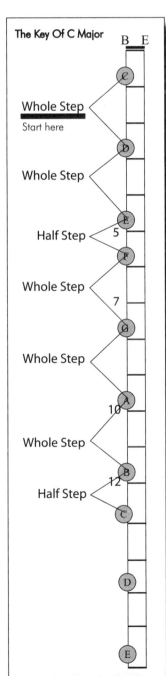

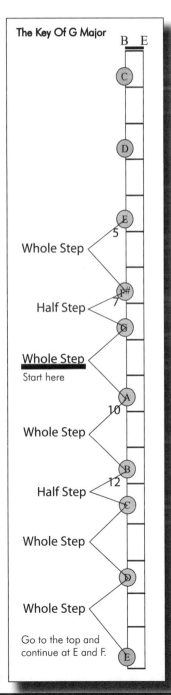

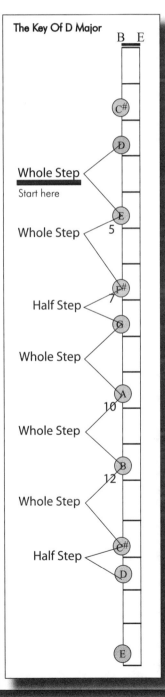

Building The Key Of C Major

We are going to examine the key of C so that we can build the chords in the key. The purpose is to show you how chords are built. You do not have to memorize this, just be sure you understand how chords are generated.

These imaginary guitar strings are tuned to the different notes of the C scale. Notice the first fret is C, D, E, F, G, A and B. We will then select every other note until we gather three notes. That is how these chords are generated. Notice the three notes in gray are C, E and G. When the middle note is four frets higher the chord will be a major chord. When it is three frets higher it will be a minor. Remember this, three frets is a minor third and four frets is a major third. It is the distance between the first and third note that determines whether the chord is major or minor. Notice the diminished chord is different than the rest. It is diminished by one half step. It is built by stacking two minor thirds. This will be fully explored in **Uncle Tim's Book Of Chords.**

Chord	C	D	E	F	G	A	B	C
Degree	1	2	3	4	5	6	7	8
Triad	Maj	Min	Min	Maj	Maj	Min	Dim	Octave
Lower Third	M	m	m	M	M	m	m	M
Upper Third	m	M	M	m	m	M	m	m

Chords Constructed Using The 1, 3 And 5 Notes

		C Major	D Minor	E Minor	F Major	G Major	A Minor	B Diminished	C Major
Root Note The tonic note of the chord		C	D	E	F	G	A	B	C
One half step from the tonic note					F			C	
One whole step from the tonic note			D	E		G	A	B	D
Third Note A minor third (shown in gray)					F	G		C	D
A major third (shown in gray)		E				A	B		E
		F	G	A		C	D	E	F
Fifth Note A diminished fifth degree (shown in gray)								B	F
A perfect fifth degree (shown in gray)		G	A	B	C	D	E		G

Building A Key

This graphic shows the construction process for the chords of this key. The three different notes are referred to as the one, three and five. They are the first note in the key, the third note in the key and the fifth note in the key. The musical notation shows this clearly. Notice we are interested in every other note. Notice we are stacking notes on top of the scale.

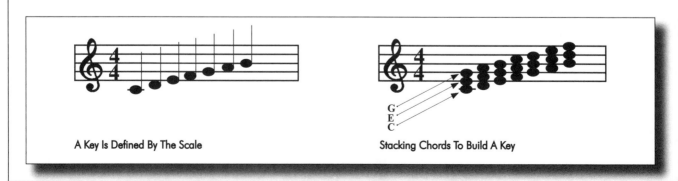

A Key Is Defined By The Scale   Stacking Chords To Build A Key

Carving Chords Out Of A Key

The first graphic contains all the notes for the first four frets.

The second fretboard contains only the notes for the key of C. These are the only notes shown on the graphic. Remember the key of C has only C, D, E, F, G, A and B. Notice these are the only notes on the second graphic.

Using the information on the last page to construct chords we will use the key of C and construct the chords by drawing lines to the notes you would play.

Notice the notes of the chords are shaded and the other notes of the key are present in white. We are using the notes of the scale, applying the rules for each chord and connecting the dots. This should point out two things very clearly. **Chords come from scales and scales contain all the information for each key.**

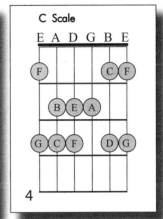

Connect The Dots

We are going to use the C scale to connect the dots for each chord. The black dots over the open strings mean do not play that note. Otherwise play all the open notes. Notice these are the same chords shown in the key of C. Do you see why playing scales makes the fretboard hand play all the notes of the key?

Chord Notes	
C major	C E G
D minor	D F A
E minor	E G B
F major	F A C
G major	G B D
A minor	A C E
B diminished	B D F

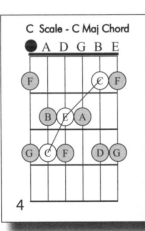

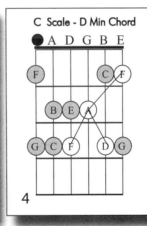

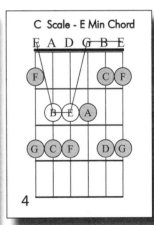

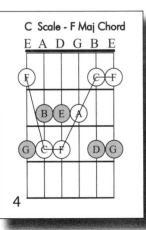

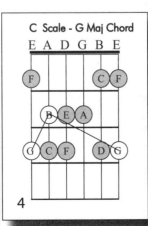

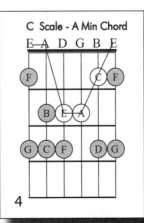

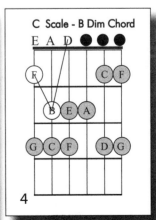

How Chords Relate To Each Other

Examining Relationships

If you look at chords in relation to what they have in common, you start to see relationships emerge. So far we have looked at chords by stacking them on the degrees of the scale. If we compare the notes in each chord, it may become apparent that some chords will share notes and sound somewhat similar.

Degree	1	2	3	4	5	6	7	8
Name	C maj	D min	E min	F maj	G maj	A min	B diminished	C major (repeat)

Degree and name of chord (not in order).

6 - A minor				A		C	E
4 - F major			F	A	C		
2 - D minor		D	F	A			
7 - B dim	B	D	F				
5 - G major	G	B	D				
3 - E minor	E	G	B				
1 - C major	C	E	G				

Notes Of Chords - Bold chords are primary chords

Notice the 1, 3 and 5 and 2, 4 and 6 are related. The 1, 3 and 5 all share the G note and the 2, 4 and 6 all share the A note. In fact each note is used three times in chords. By examining chords in this way we can see which chords share the same notes. We can now diagram the relationships between chords that occur because of the shared notes.

The Primary Chords. The primary chords are the 1, 4 and 5. They are the major chords in the major key (they are the minor chords in a minor key). They are considered primary because they are a fifth above and below tonic and they are the same kind of chord as tonic (major). From tonic you can travel a fifth above and arrive at the 5th chord or you can travel a fifth below tonic and arrive at the 4th chord. Either way you go, tonic is a fifth away and this creates a relationship.

Secondary Chords. These are the minor and diminished chords in the major key. A secondary chord can be substituted for any primary chord with which it shares two notes.

Fourths and Fifths

We need to look at an extended scale so that we may understand what a fifth above tonic is compared to a fifth below tonic. In this example notice that five degrees above C is the note of G, which is the fifth degree. It is five degrees higher than C. Now notice what note is five degrees above F. The answer is C. F is the fourth degree above C but it is also five degrees behind C. Notice the fourth and fifth are the same distance away from tonic. These are the primary chords.

The Primary Chords

Degree	1	2	3	4	5	6	7	1	2	3	4	5	6	7	1
Name	C	D	E	F	G	A	B	C	D	E	F	G	A	B	C

The Secondary Chords

Degree	1	2	3	4	5	6	7	1	2	3	4	5	6	7	1
Name	C	D	E	F	G	A	B	C	D	E	F	G	A	B	C

Notice the E minor shares two notes with both C major and G major. A minor shares two notes with F major and C major. Notice B dim shares two notes with G major and D minor. Everything is related.

Chords And Keys

The Relationships In The Key

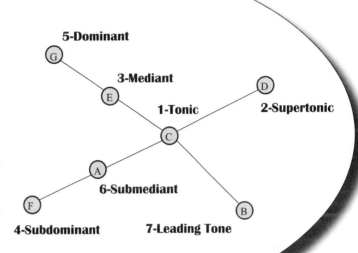

Common Notes

Notice the tonic note is in the center of the graphic. Everything in the key of C relates most strongly to C. Also notice the 5 chord and the 4 chord are off in their own direction. The 3 chord is halfway between the 1 and 5 chords. The 6 chord shares two notes with both the 1 and 4 chords. The 2 chord shares two notes with the 7 chord and the 4 chord.

5-Dominant
3-Mediant
1-Tonic
2-Supertonic
6-Submediant
4-Subdominant
7-Leading Tone

Progressing Through A Key

There are some simple rules that can be applied to every key. Each degree has a unique personality. The degrees will behave the same across keys and certain personality traits of each degree will always be present in every key. This is one of the reasons we practice the chords in every key. As you play them you get to know them. As you play through every key you begin to hear and understand the differences and similarities. Even though we can talk about and begin to understand chords, talking about it cannot provide the same experience as playing the chords and getting to know them over time. Here are some characteristics concerning each degree that will apply to every key.

1 - Tonic. Always the chord that will bring a piece to rest. This chord will resolve the music and bring it to rest. All chords relate to tonic. When you end a simple song, you usually do so with the tonic chord or note.

3 - Mediant. Located between tonic and the dominant chord, this chord can be used to transition to tonic from the dominant chord. It will sound similar to both chords because it shares two notes with each.

5 - Dominant. The dominant chord is almost opposite to tonic. It also seeks resolution towards tonic. The dominant is constructed on a perfect fifth above tonic. From tonic it is a fifth to the dominant position. Going to the dominant from tonic is a strong move and creates a distinct direction to the music.

2 - Supertonic. The closest chord to tonic (as with the diminished chord). It will share two notes with the subdominant.

4 - Subdominant. Like the dominant chord the subdominant chord is built on a perfect fifth. From the fourth to tonic is a fifth. Going to the subdominant from tonic is also a strong move.

6 - Submediant. This is halfway between the fourth and tonic. It shares two notes with tonic and this forms a very unique relationship with tonic. It is the relative minor of tonic. The relative minor uses the same notes for the relative minor key. The relative minor key is very close to tonic. Often times you cannot tell the difference because the notes are the same.

7 - Diminished. The most unstable chord in the group. The diminished chord will demand movement usually towards tonic (since it is so close). This chord makes you feel like you need to move to another chord. It is good at inserting tension. This tension can be hard to manage and that is one of the reasons why we do not use it much yet. Remember that every chord will add a unique bit of interest if used in the right setting. You can use any of these chords in a progression and experimenting with them will tell you what you like. There are always new ways to combine them to do something different. Experiment!

The Key Of C Major

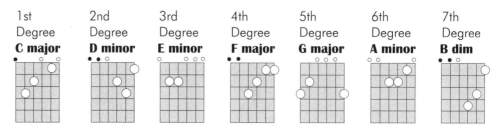

1st Degree	2nd Degree	3rd Degree	4th Degree	5th Degree	6th Degree	7th Degree
C major	D minor	E minor	F major	G major	A minor	B dim

These are the chords of the key of C major. It is common to see all of them used in songs with the exception of the diminished chord. Since it is so unstable (and has a diminished sound) it is used less frequently. Keep in mind it has some very good usages that you may explore later.

The Degrees Of A Key

This is the palette for songs. What we are really doing when we transpose is swap the chords of the same degree in different keys. We have talked about substitution of different chords in the same key, but now we are concerned with changing keys and using the same degree.

Transposing To Another Key

Here is an example of changing keys. The keys in this example are C, G and D. If you are playing C, G and F you are playing the chords based on the one, five and four degrees of the C scale. See the example above. You can transpose to another key by choosing the chords based on the one, five and four degree in that key.

Here are three examples of switching keys using the same degrees. I have included all twelve keys laid out in this fashion. That should serve as a chord guide for each key as well as a guide for transposing. You will also see another chart that will add a seventh degree to each chord. You may not be able to make sense of this yet, but you will in a little while.

	Keynote 1st Degree	2nd Degree	3rd Degree	4th Degree	5th Degree	6th Degree	7th Degree
The Key Of C	C major	D minor	E minor	F major	G major	A minor	B dim
The Key Of G	G major	A minor	B minor	C major	D major	E minor	F# dim
The Key Of D	D major	E minor	F# minor	G major	A major	B minor	C# dim

The Key Of C Major

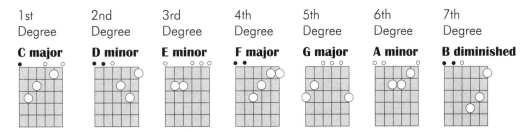

	1st Degree	2nd Degree	3rd Degree	4th Degree	5th Degree	6th Degree	7th Degree
	C major	D minor	E minor	F major	G major	A minor	B diminished

The key of A minor is an extension of the key of C. Nothing is different but the starting point. Instead of progressing C, D, E, F, G, A and B, we go A, B, C, D, E, F and G. Notice none of the notes are sharped. If you are playing the notes of C you are playing the notes of A minor. The chords are the same too.

The Key Of A Minor

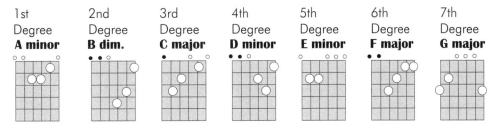

	1st Degree	2nd Degree	3rd Degree	4th Degree	5th Degree	6th Degree	7th Degree
	A minor	B dim.	C major	D minor	E minor	F major	G major

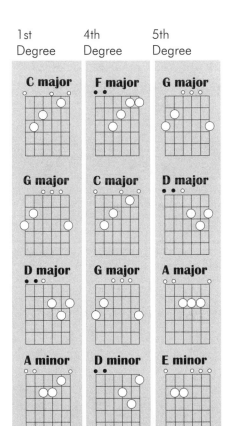

1st Degree	4th Degree	5th Degree
C major	F major	G major
G major	C major	D major
D major	G major	A major
A minor	D minor	E minor

Notice the chords in the key of A minor are the same as for C major. The location is different because we changed the starting point. Remember the starting note is now A. If you were to transpose the previous example into the key of A minor, you would play the chords for the one four and five degrees of the scale. Each progression in each key is shown here. The degrees stay the same, the progression is still a one, four, five but the chords have been substituted according to the degrees of the scale for each key.

For the key of C the passage is   C major, F major, G major
For the key of G the passage is   G major, C major, D major
For the key of D the passage is   D major, G major, A major
For the key of A minor it is   A minor, D minor, E minor

Each passage contains a one, four and five degrees for each key. This is an example of the relevance of keys. There are many different things that can be pointed out here. Some of it can get quite complicated. At the beginner level be aware that transposition can be as easy as these examples. Becoming advanced in a subject like music often times means learning what you already know in greater detail.

As you play you will have need to transpose sooner or later, particularly when you play a song with someone who only knows that song in a different key. This is one of the thought processes that shapes your knowledge of keys, theory and practical application.

Chord Chart

The Key Of C	C major	D minor	E minor	F major	G major	A minor	B dim
The Key Of G	G major	A minor	B minor	C major	D major	E minor	F# dim
The Key Of D	D major	E minor	F# minor	G major	A major	B minor	C# dim
The Key Of A	A major	B minor	C# minor	D major	E major	F# minor	G# dim
The Key Of E	E major	F# minor	G# minor	A major	B major	C# minor	D# dim
The Key Of B	B major	C# minor	D# minor	E major	F# major	G# minor	A# dim
The Key Of F#	F# major	G# minor	A# minor	B major	C# major	D# minor	E# dim
The Key Of C#	C# major	D# minor	E# minor	F# major	G# major	A# minor	B# dim
The Key Of Ab	Ab major	Bb minor	C minor	Db major	Eb major	F minor	G dim
The Key Of Eb	Eb major	F minor	G minor	Ab major	Bb major	C minor	D dim
The Key Of Bb	Bb major	C minor	D minor	Eb major	F major	G minor	A dim
The Key Of F	F major	G minor	A minor	Bb major	C major	D minor	E dim

The Key Of C — C maj 7 | D min 7 | E min 7 | F maj 7 | G 7 | A min 7 | B dim 7

The Key Of G — G maj 7 | A min 7 | B min 7 | C maj 7 | D 7 | E min 7 | F# dim 7

The Key Of D — D maj 7 | E min 7 | F# min 7 | G maj 7 | A 7 | B min 7 | C# dim 7

The Key Of A — A maj 7 | B min 7 | C# min 7 | D maj 7 | E 7 | F# min 7 | G# dim 7

The Key Of E — E maj 7 | F# min 7 | G# min 7 | A maj 7 | B 7 | C# min 7 | D# dim 7

The Key Of B — B maj 7 | C# min 7 | D# min 7 | E maj 7 | F# 7 | G# min 7 | A# dim 7

The Key Of F# — F# maj 7 | G# min 7 | A# min 7 | B maj 7 | C# 7 | D# min 7 | E# dim 7

The Key Of C# — C# maj 7 | D# min 7 | E# min 7 | F# maj 7 | G# 7 | A# min 7 | C dim 7

The Key Of Ab — Ab maj 7 | Bb min 7 | C min 7 | Db maj 7 | Eb 7 | F min 7 | G dim 7

The Key Of Eb — Eb maj 7 | F min 7 | G min 7 | Ab maj 7 | Bb 7 | C min 7 | D dim 7

The Key Of Bb — Bb maj 7 | C min 7 | D min 7 | Eb maj 7 | F 7 | G min 7 | A dim 7

The Key Of F — F maj 7 | G min 7 | A min 7 | Bb maj 7 | C 7 | D min 7 | E dim 7

Are We Done Yet?

What have we done? What does this information give us? Later on we will tie this into the big picture and expose exactly what this information can do for you. You know much more than you think you know. By the way, we are never done. There are many paths to take and many musical things to explore.

The complete diatonic information code. The next time you are playing a song, you have all the tools to determine what key it is in. Slide up the E string until you hear the tonic note of the song. Run the scale for the key. Often you will know instantly when you hit the tonic note. You will hear the ringing of the key and the tonic note will sound much more correct than the other notes. If the scale sounds correct but the tonic note does not bring it to rest, go to the relative minor note and see if that note serves as tonic. If it does you are in the minor key.

Once you have the key, you can prepare for many things. If it is a song you are trying to learn, you can concentrate on the chords of the key and anticipate what chords will come next. You can then analyze the progression, learning what makes up the type of song you like. You then have a recipe for creating your own. If you want to learn the lead line, it will most likely be carved out from the scale. Knowing this will help you train your ear. Your ear will come to recognize changes and contrasting melodies among other things. The complete diatonic information code will be used in every song you are likely to play. In the advanced songs, it will disguise itself and take different shapes.

Reread what you have just learned. Everything will make better sense the second time!

These keys and the left and right hand technical work will signal the end of the first year's requirement for basic study. This is the foundation! From here I have a suggestion. The next section contains chords and scales based on what you know. These are not advanced chords in that they are located in or close to the first position, however they use more complex fingerings. They also expand the notes used in building chords to include seventh chords. These are chords that can be substituted for the common chords at the drop of a hat. They will add new combinations on top of the forms already played.

In addition to chords we will introduce a new scale formula, the pentatonic scale. The pentatonic scale is based on the diatonic scale, it is a simpler scale because it contains only five notes not seven. It is contained inside the diatonic and has very close associations. It is the backbone of rock lead guitar and combined with the seventh chords will provide advanced training to your fingers and mind. It is the first step out of the beginner stage. The pentatonic scales will work with the chords and keys you have just memorized as well as the new chords.

Are You A Beginner?

If you have played everything in the book over a period of eight or more months almost every day and you have a reasonable understanding both mentally and physically, you are no longer a beginner! If you have done that, you did not need me to tell you this, you already knew! By the way, do your hands hurt?

The Pentatonic Keys

Scales And Chords
For The First Position Pentatonic Keys

The Pentatonic Keys

In some musical styles the pentatonic keys are very important. If you are going to play rock music, these are the scales that will be used most often. You can always use the diatonic scales too. They are somewhat interchangeable. The pentatonic keys are actually a subset of the diatonic keys. Some instructors teach these first, although, I believe it is better to have a clear understanding of diatonic keys first. Everything is built on the diatonic scales. After you can hear the pentatonic scale and are familiar with the typical diatonic scale, you can tell the difference between the two scale types.

The pentatonic scales can be played over the typical chords presented in the diatonic keys. In addition, it is advisable to learn some seventh chords. They can change the feeling of a piece of music when substituted for the basic chords already learned.

These scales and chords are well beyond the beginner level. They are more complex and provide options beyond the basics. By playing the diatonic keys and then the pentatonic keys you can get a distinct feeling of the differences between the two. Do not be afraid to experiment with both.

C Pentatonic Scale And 7th Chords

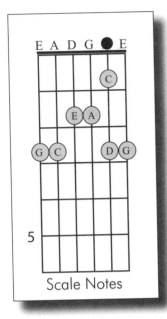

Scale Notes

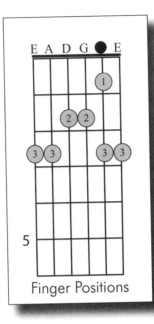

Finger Positions

The Scale of C Pentatonic. As with the diatonic scales use the finger chart to play these scales. The fingerings will be noticeably different than the diatonics.

The pentatonic scale for C will use the 1, 2, 3, 5 and 6 degrees of the diatonic scale. Remember the notes will be C, D, E, G and A. The F and B are omitted. This is the formula for pentatonic scales.

Finger Positions
1 = Index Finger
2 = Second Finger
3 = Ring Finger
4 = Pinky

Seventh Chords. Just like the chords shown in the diatonic section, these chords are based on the one, three and five of the scale, however we are now adding the seventh degree. This will change the sound because of the added seventh. The introduction of seventh chords with pentatonic scales is complimentary. You can play the same progressions as before, but now you can substitute these chords for the ones already learned. The pentatonic scales can serve as a palette for lead construction when used with these chords. So can the diatonic scale, however it may take more work to make it sound correct.

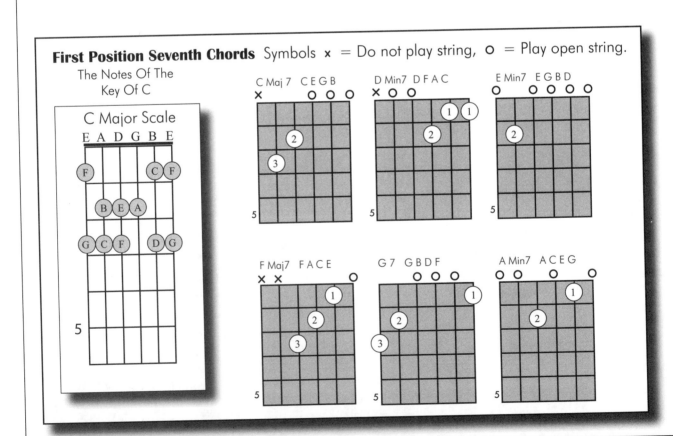

First Position Seventh Chords Symbols **x** = Do not play string, **o** = Play open string.

The Notes Of The Key Of C

C Major Scale

The Scale of G Pentatonic. Since you are playing five notes instead of seven, this can be easier. Often times the seventh degree of the diatonic scale can be an awkward note. As with the fourth note the pentatonic scale automatically eliminates the seventh degree.

The pentatonic scale can be used to construct lead lines. The spacing of these five notes will allow for easier construction of melodies. The notes are spread out and the bigger spacing means they do not relate to each other as strongly. As a consequence, it does not sound as much like a linear scale.

Seventh Chords. Notice the basic chord form is the same as the G major chords. These chords are a part of G major and are derived from the basic chords. They should look similar. Notice the pattern of major and minor chords is carried over. The reason we use major sevenths and seventh chords as we do is so we do not violate the key. These seventh notes fall within the scale. There are seventh chords that do not. That is an advanced subject. After you get the feeling of these chords you may want to look at the other seventh chords. Later!

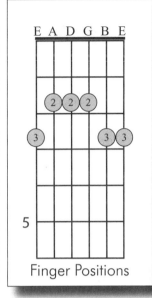

Scale Notes | Finger Positions

Degree	1	2	3	4	5	6	7
Diatonic scale notes	G	A	B	C	D	E	F#
Pentatonic scale notes	G	A	B		D	E	

First Position Seventh Chords Symbols **x** = Do not play string, **o** = Play open string.

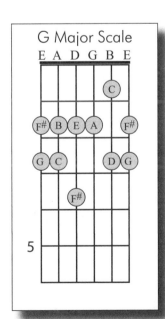

G Major Scale

G Maj7 G B D F#

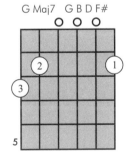

A Min7 A C E G

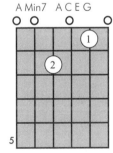

B Min7 B D F# A

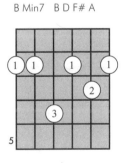

C Maj7 C E G B

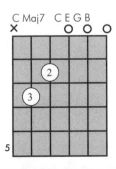

D 7 D F# A C

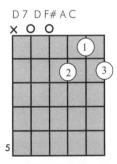

E Min7 E G B D

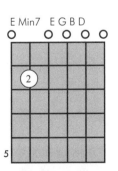

D Pentatonic Scale And 7th Chords

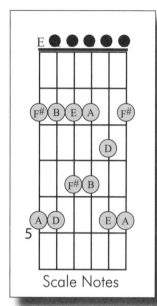

Scale Notes

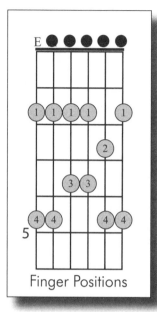

Finger Positions

The Scale of D Pentatonic. Have you noticed a markedly different feeling with the pentatonic scales. The notes are at least a whole step apart and there are step and a half intervals.

Let's look at the spacing of the pentatonic scale. Starting with the key note.

Between D and E Whole step
Between E and F# Whole step
Between F# and A Whole step and one half step
Between A and B Whole step
Between B and D Whole step and one half step

The spacing is different and that is why the sound of the scale is so different.

Seventh Chords. These chords are harder to play than the basic chords of the key. You are playing four different notes instead of three different notes. If you have played the basic chords in the previous section, these should seem familiar. They are based on those same chords most of the time. They work the same repeatable way and usually have the root in the same position. If you can associate the root note with the chord, you will start to understand how these chords are built from the note. A good example is the F# minor 7 chord below. The root note is the F# note on the second fret of the E string. If you use the G note for the root (move the chord up one fret), the chord becomes a G minor 7. The chord can be used by any note on that string and become the minor 7 chord for whatever note you choose.

Degree	1	2	3	4	5	6	7
Diatonic scale notes	D	E	F#	G	A	B	C#
Pentatonic scale notes	D	E	F#		A	B	

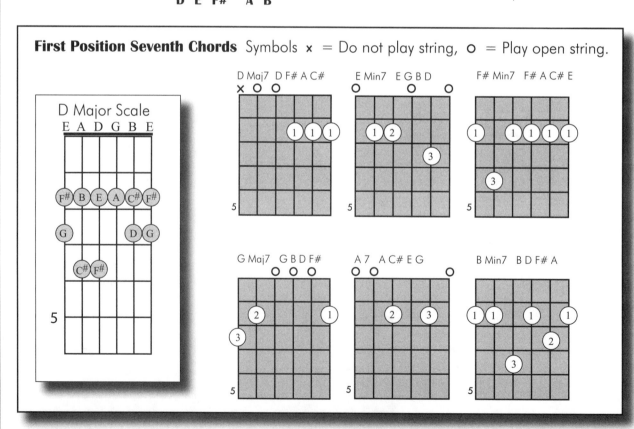

First Position Seventh Chords Symbols **x** = Do not play string, **o** = Play open string.

D Major Scale

D Maj7 D F# A C#
E Min7 E G B D
F# Min7 F# A C# E
G Maj7 G B D F#
A 7 A C# E G
B Min7 B D F# A

Page 76

A Pentatonic Scale And 7th Chords

The Scale of A Pentatonic. In this example we are turning our back on the open string notes. We could use the E, A and B but they are not so convenient. This brings up an important point, you can alter these scales to include different locations of the same note. In other words you could omit the B note in the G string and play the open string B instead. In many cases it would be too awkward, however in the right situation it may highlight some creative choice. The important thing to get is that you can mix things up as long as you obey the rules.

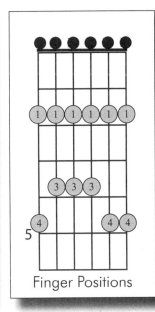

Scale Notes   Finger Positions

Degree	1	2	3	4	5	6	7
Diatonic scale notes	A	B	C#	D	E	F#	G#
Pentatonic scale notes	A	B	C#		E	F#	

Seventh Chords. If you are starting to hear the familiar sound of the key of A as well as the distinct flavor of the inclusion of the seventh interval, you are piecing together the fabric of keys. Mentally this will help you to hear the boundaries of a key and understand how it works as an entity. This is a very big mental picture, it will take time to understand it and know how to use it. This material is the front line of the tonal concept.

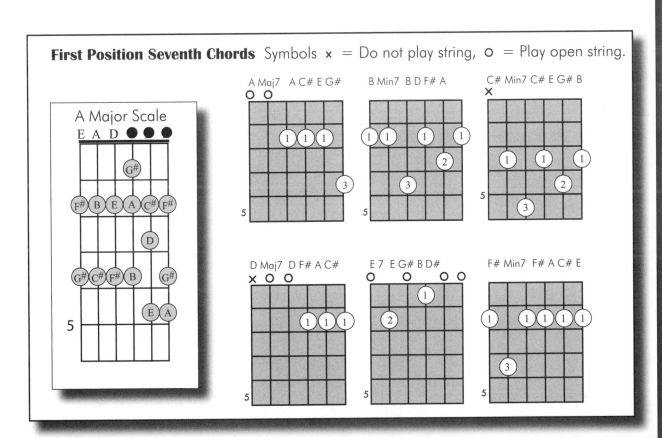

First Position Seventh Chords Symbols ✗ = Do not play string, ○ = Play open string.

A Major Scale

A Maj7   A C# E G#

B Min7   B D F# A

C# Min7 C# E G# B

D Maj7   D F# A C#

E 7   E G# B D#

F# Min7 F# A C# E

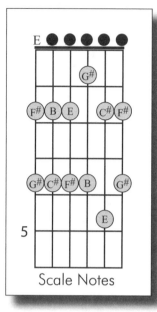

Scale Notes

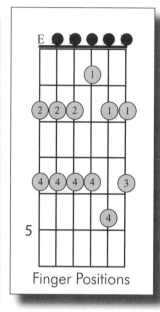

Finger Positions

The Scale of E Pentatonic. Let's compare the spacing of E major pentatonic to D major pentatonic.

Key of D

Between D and E   Whole step
Between E and F#   Whole step
Between F# and A   Whole step and one half step
Between A and B   Whole step
Between B and D   Whole step and one half step

Key of E

Between E and F#   Whole step
Between F# and G# Whole step
Between G# and B   Whole step and one half step
Between B and C#   Whole step
Between C# and E   Whole step and one half step

Notice the spacing is the exact same just like the diatonic keys. This is the signature spacing of pentatonic scales. They will all be this way. The diatonic

and pentatonic scales are very closely related.

Seventh Chords. Remember two things are going on at the same time on this page. We are building seventh chords in diatonic keys, however we are playing pentatonic scales. The chords are in diatonic keys. The pentatonic scale is also built from a diatonic scale.

Degree	1	2	3	4	5	6	7
Diatonic scale notes	E	F#	G#	A	B	C#	D#
Pentatonic scale notes	E	F#	G#		B	C#	

First Position Seventh Chords Symbols   x   = Do not play string,   o   = Play open string.

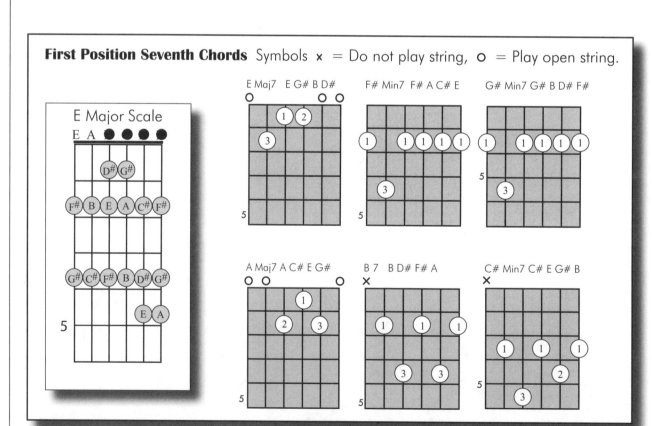

The Scale of B Pentatonic. This fingering is one of my favorites. I use this one all over the neck. The root note on the A string serves as a reference when you start moving it up and down.

Why have we chosen to learn the diatonic scale first, then the pentatonic? The biggest reason is to show the entire key first. If you learn bits and pieces every time you learn something new about the key, you will wonder how much more there is to know. It seems like it never ends. This way you see the big picture and can then concentrate on working within the picture. It's easier!

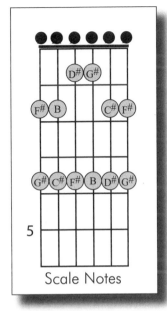

Scale Notes

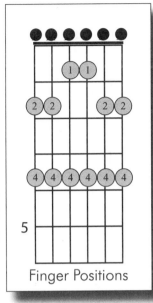

Finger Positions

Degree	1	2	3	4	5	6	7
Diatonic scale notes	B	C#	D#	E	F#	G#	A#
Pentatonic scale notes	B	C#	D#		F#	G#	

Seventh Chords. By now you have left the beginning stages and are learning more difficult chords. Are you reaping the reward of playing these slowly and cleanly? These chords are very full bodied and rich. As you play each chord do you hear the sound of the scale? Can you tell you are climbing through the key? Can you hear the new flavor of an additional seventh note in the scale?

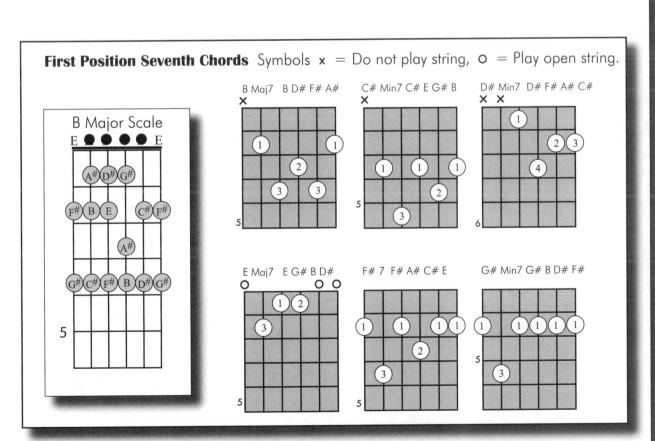

First Position Seventh Chords Symbols x = Do not play string, O = Play open string.

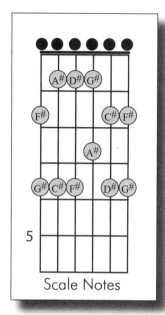

Scale Notes

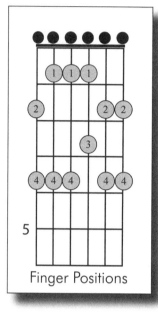

Finger Positions

The Scale of F# Pentatonic. You may want to consider adding different fingerings to these scales. The choice of which fingers to use will eventually be determined by what you are going to play next. If you are going to climb up the neck, you may choose to use the 1 and 3 fingers for the notes on the B and E strings.

One finger for each fret works really well for the pentatonic scales, but not always. These are two note per string scales, which are usually compact. However there are different pathways you can travel and they will not always be constructed of small spans. As you experiment and play more music, you will stumble upon the need to play these differently.

Seventh Chords. These chords are going to require you to play new configurations. We have not seen the form used for the F# Maj 7 chord before. Stretching your fingers evenly will require new concentration. Remember to keep your thumb on the ridge of the neck, it will make playing this chord easier.

Degree	1	2	3	4	5	6	7
Diatonic scale notes	F#	G#	A#	B	C#	D#	E#
Pentatonic scale notes	F#	G#	A#		C#	D#	

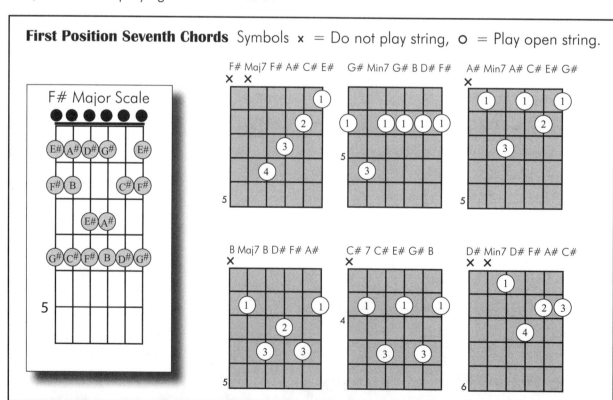

First Position Seventh Chords Symbols x = Do not play string, o = Play open string.

F# Major Scale

F# Maj7 F# A# C# E#

G# Min7 G# B D# F#

A# Min7 A# C# E# G#

B Maj7 B D# F# A#

C# 7 C# E# G# B

D# Min7 D# F# A# C#

The Scale of C# Pentatonic. This fingering is another of my favorites. If your hand is getting fatigued, this type of compressed scale can allow you to keep practicing because the hand does not have to stretch as far.

Although I do not play C# pentatonic as much as other keys, there are vital reasons to play in this key. Much of those reasons lie ahead of you. It will become important as you continue to learn. One reason is that this same pattern can slide up one fret to become a D major pentatonic which is a key that you will probably use quite a bit.

Seventh Chords. Once again we use the same chord forms. If you see the basic chord forms in these chords you are well on your way to a deep understanding of music and the guitar. You know most of the rules, now it is a matter of seeing the rules in action. That will happen as you play and it will become more and more important as you get better.

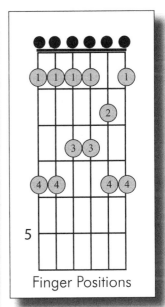

Scale Notes   Finger Positions

Degree	1	2	3	4	5	6	7
Diatonic scale notes	C#	D#	E#	F#	G#	A#	B#
Pentatonic scale notes	C#	D#	E#		G#	A#	

First Position Seventh Chords Symbols **x** = Do not play string, **o** = Play open string.

C# Major Scale

C #Maj7 C# E# G# B#

D #Min7 D# F# A# C#

E# Min7 E# G# B# D#

F #Maj7 F# A# C# E#

G #7 G# B# D# F#

A #Min7 A# C# E# G#

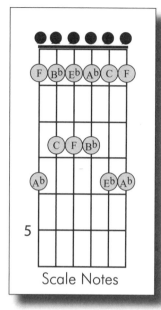

Scale Notes

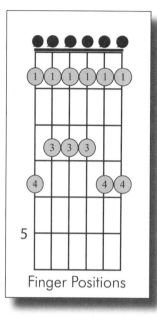

Finger Positions

The Scale of Ab Pentatonic. Once again the two note per string scale facilitates the one finger per fret concept.

Some teachers teach the pentatonic scale before the diatonic scale because you do not have to deal with the seventh degree. Keep in mind in the diatonic key, the seventh degree is always sharp (except C major). This will keep it one half step behind tonic. As stated before this is an unstable relationship by design. Since it is sharp, it provides the sense of motion to tonic. It is so close yet not tonic. Part of developing taste as a lead line generator is dealing with the seventh degree

of the diatonic scale. The pentatonic scales have a way of dealing with the seventh degree of the major scale, they don't!

Degree	1	2	3	4	5	6	7
Diatonic scale notes	Ab	Bb	C	Db	Eb	F	G
Pentatonic scale notes	Ab	Bb	C		Eb	F	

Seventh Chords. Now think about this. With the pentatonic scale we avoid the awkward seventh degree. When building seventh chords we include it in every chord. In these instances it provides a distinct flavor and contributes to a jazzy feeling. Part of an advanced understanding of keys revolves around this funny note. This will also take time.

First Position Seventh Chords Symbols **x** = Do not play string, **o** = Play open string.

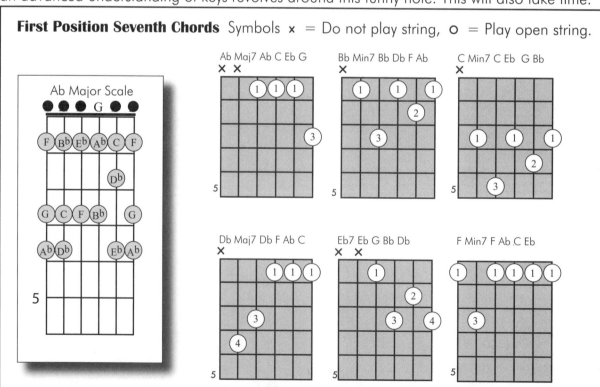

The Scale of Eb Pentatonic. As with the diatonic keys, we start to gain the open string notes as we get close to the key of C. In the key of Eb it presents an awkward situation. Notice the G string is now supplying the G note rather than picking it up on the fifth fret of the D string. You can play it there, but you must then stretch to play it because you will be playing three notes per string. Open strings are usually easy to play because you just play an open string. But as you are rolling along with a scale that does not use

Degree	1	2	3	4	5	6	7
Diatonic scale notes	Eb	F	G	Ab	Bb	C	D
Pentatonic scale notes	Eb	F	G		Bb	C	

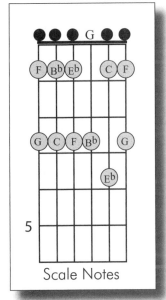

Scale Notes

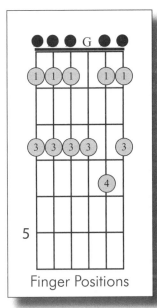

Finger Positions

open strings and then you insert one, it can be hard to execute. It requires that you do not touch the strings as it is sounding. It is common to have trouble hitting an open string note when you have not been using them.

Seventh Chords. We recycle a lot of chord forms to make these chords. We use the same forms in most keys, we just move the position. If you have learned to play them at one location, all you have to do is get used to the spacing of the frets. Remember frets are not evenly spaced, the closer you get to the body of the guitar, the closer the spacing becomes.

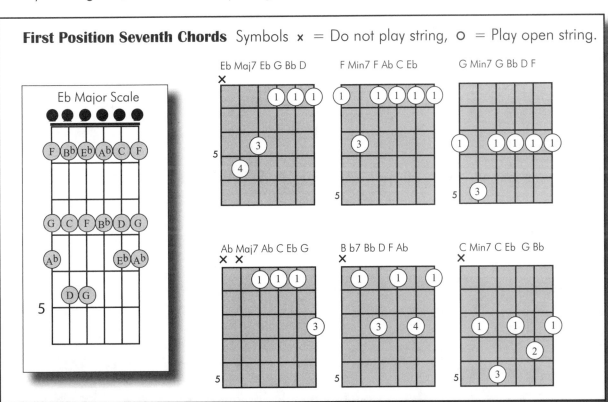

First Position Seventh Chords Symbols **x** = Do not play string, **o** = Play open string.

Eb Major Scale

Eb Maj7 Eb G Bb D

F Min7 F Ab C Eb

G Min7 G Bb D F

Ab Maj7 Ab C Eb G

B b7 Bb D F Ab

C Min7 C Eb G Bb

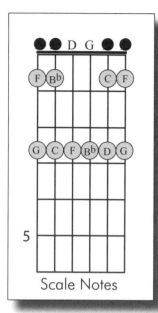

Scale Notes

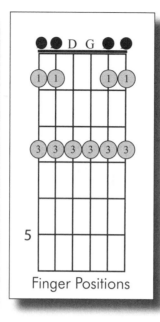

Finger Positions

The Scale of Bb Pentatonic. Test yourself on how well you know this material. Can you play this scale with your eyes closed? Can you play this scale and then the diatonic version of it? Can you identify the key note by running the scale and ending on it? Can you play it without muting any notes or making others buzz? Do you recognize this pattern as the same one you played in the key of B? The only difference is we have moved it back one fret and in so doing we have incorporated the open string D and G notes. There are two

Degree	1	2	3	4	5	6	7
Diatonic scale notes	Bb	C	D	Eb	F	G	A
Pentatonic scale notes	Bb	C	D		F	G	

ways to know this, mentally and physically. Physically, it is the ability to pick up a guitar and play this without mistakes. Mentally, it is knowing what notes to play. You can get confused and disoriented both mentally and physically. You must be able to control both to control this information. Like everything else it will take time.

Seventh Chords. After you play these, can you then close your eyes and play them from memory? Can you determine the root note for every chord? Can you slide the chord form up a few frets and sound the chord correctly?

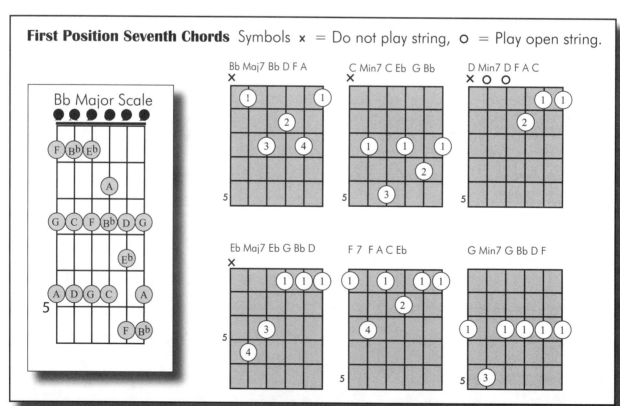

First Position Seventh Chords Symbols x = Do not play string, o = Play open string.

Bb Major Scale

Bb Maj7 Bb D F A

C Min7 C Eb G Bb

D Min7 D F A C

Eb Maj7 Eb G Bb D

F 7 F A C Eb

G Min7 G Bb D F

F Pentatonic Scale And 7th Chords

The Scale of F Pentatonic. This is the final stop for scales. You have now seen diatonic and pentatonic scales for the first position. The rules you have learned will come up time and time again. Now that you have learned them you know the hardest part. It can be remarkably easy to understand the entire fretboard now. You have been prepared for this. You have learned much of what you need to go farther.

Seventh Chords. Let this information work for awhile without trying to learn anything new. You have been continuing to build on top of the knowledge you have acquired since you started. Now just let it sink in for awhile. This will help you to use it and continue to understand it.

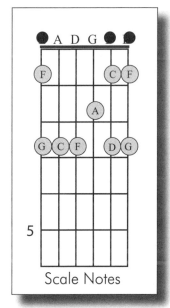

Scale Notes

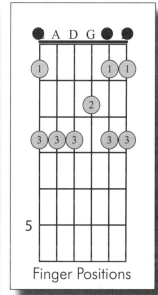

Finger Positions

Degree	1	2	3	4	5	6	7
Diatonic scale notes	F	G	A	Bb	C	D	E
Pentatonic scale notes	F	G	A		C	D	

First Position Seventh Chords Symbols **x** = Do not play string, **o** = Play open string.

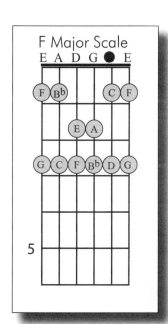

F Major Scale

F Maj7   F A C E

G Min7 G Bb D F

A Min7   A C E G

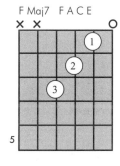
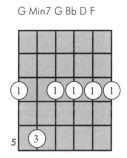
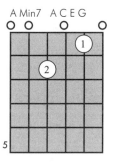

Bb Maj7 Bb D F A

C7   C E G Bb

D Min7 D F A C

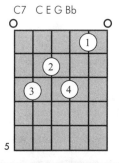

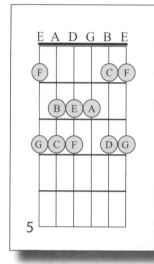

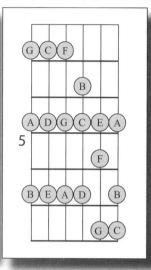

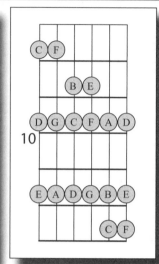

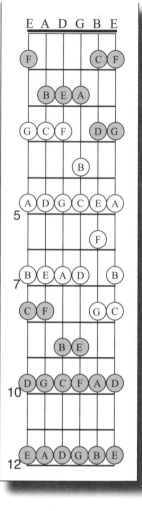

Advance Fretboard Concepts

You have been secretly set up to know all your scales in every position, for every key without any more memorization! You have practiced several different scale patterns for the first position scales, three of which are shown above. As you already know, the diagram to the right is the entire set of notes in the key of C.

Notice all three patterns shown above are contained right on top of each other in the diagram to the right. Also notice the position of each pattern has been moved to a new part of the fretboard.

Think about this! You know the diagram to the right contains the entire key of C. Everything in the key of C is in this diagram. You already know the scale patterns, and if you play them as shown here you will be playing in the key of C. If you memorize them on top of each other as shown, you are in effect memorizing the entire key of C. This is a very easy way to envision the entire key of C and you already have memorized it!

Lets take it one step further! Look at the diagrams below. Notice it starts with the key of C as discussed above. But also notice the same pattern is used in the next key which is C#. The exact same pattern has been moved up one fret and is now the next key. Move it up one more fret and it becomes the key of D.

You are now in position to know every scale in every key for the entire fretboard. Most of the hard work has been done. Now you just have to link a few concepts and your foundation will expand to cover the entire fretboard. It may take awhile for this to sink in, it is an enormous jump in scope. You have been preparing for this all along.

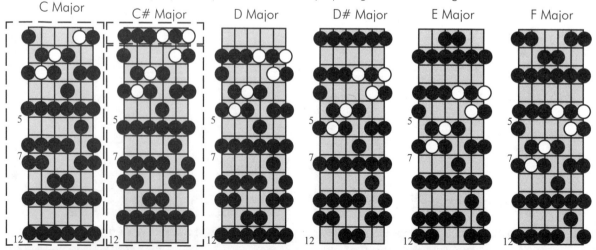

C Major   C# Major   D Major   D# Major   E Major   F Major

All The Chords For C Major Are In Here!

The white dots are a C chord. Do you see it in every example below? Have you noticed when you play the chords in each key, you were only using the notes in the scale. You never played a chord that was not contained in the scale. The scale contains the notes of the key and that is what is available to make the chords of the key.

The same thing will work in this twelve fret pattern. This twelve fret pattern contains only the notes in the key. If you form the chords for the key of C over the entire fretboard they will all fit in this pattern. Remember the scale contains only the notes of the key and the chords are made up of the notes in the key.

This becomes a valuable tool once you build up your mental chord library. When you fit the keys together, you expand your limits of what is possible. This is a very advanced and very reachable concept!

Anything You Learn In One Key Is Available In Every Key!

This is a very important concept. It is often overlooked as a way to make things easier. Over time you will have need to be familiar with several different keys. Even simple rock and roll songs are often played in the keys of C, G, D, A and E. If you learn a progression of chords in one key, you can play it in any of these keys. This may become necessary if a singer needs to transpose into a key more favorable for their vocal range. This approach is also very helpful when trying to write songs. You can identify what worked for artists you like and write similar progressions or work out new concepts in the same keys. There are more reasons to learn this than we have time to discuss.

Uncle Tim's Building Blocks Is The Next Step!

You can get a complete understanding of scales for the entire fretboard in the next book in the series. It builds this advanced understanding on top of the foundation you acquired in this book. It will use these same graphics to totally map the fretboard. It will help you to understand the whole fretboard and become comfortable using it. Once you learn how to play, most people are playing either chords or scales (or parts based on these two). Lead lines can be traced back to scales and progressions are usually based on chords (in part). **Uncle Tim's Building Blocks** will completely explore scales and **Uncle Tim's Book Of Chords** will explore chords. Together they will completely map the fretboard for chords and scales.

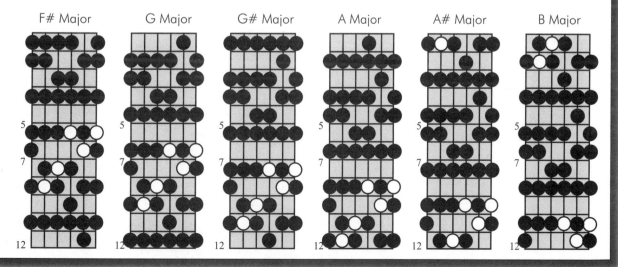